VOICE AND VERSE

A STUDY IN
ENGLISH SONG

BY

H. C. COLLES

Copyright © 2013 Read Books Ltd.
This book is copyright and may not be
reproduced or copied in any way without
the express permission of the publisher in writing

British Library Cataloguing-in-Publication Data
A catalogue record for this book is available from the
British Library

A Short History of Musical Notation

Musical Notation is any system used to visually represent aurally perceived music through the use of written symbols – including ancient or modern musical symbols. Although many ancient cultures used symbols to represent melodies, none of these systems are nearly as comprehensive as written language, limiting knowledge of ancient music to a few fragments. Although it has incredibly old roots, comprehensive music notation only began to be developed in Europe in the Middle Ages but has since been adapted to many kinds of music worldwide.

The earliest form of musical notation can be found in a cuneiform tablet that was created at Nippur, in today's Iraq around 2000 BC. The tablet represents fragmentary instructions for performing music, that the music was composed in harmonies of thirds, and that it was written in a diatonic scale. A tablet from about 1250 BC shows a more developed form of notation, and though the interpretation of the system is still controversial, it is clear that the notation indicates the names of strings on a lyre. Although fragmentary, these tablets represent the earliest notated melodies found anywhere in the world.

The ancient Greeks used musical notation from at least the sixth century BC until approximately the fourth century AD, and several complete compositions and fragments using this notation survive. This system consisted of symbols placed above text syllables, and the Delphic Hyms, dated to the second century BC use this notation – but are not completely preserved. Such methods appear to have fallen out of use around the time of the Decline of the Roman Empire. The Byzantine Empire was the other major civilisation to use musical notation, and theirs was remarkably similar to subsequent Western notation, in that it was ordered left to right, and separated into measures. The main difference is that the Byzantine notation symbols were *differential* rather than absolute, i.e. they indicate pitch *change* (rise or fall), and the musician had to deduce correctly, from the score and the note they were singing, which note came next.

In early Europe, a rough form of notation for remembering Gregorian chants was established, but the problem with this system was that it only showed melodic contours – and consequently the music could not be read by someone who did not know the tune. To address the issue of exact pitch, a staff was introduced consisting originally of a single horizontal line, but this was progressively extended until a system of four parallel, horizontal lines was standardized. This is traditionally attributed to **Guido of Arezzo**, who set out his thoughts on the changes in his first musical treatise, *Micrologus* (1026). The modern five-line staff was first adopted in France and became almost universal by the sixteenth century (although the use of staves with other numbers of lines was still widespread well into the seventeenth century).

As is evident from this incredibly short and potted history, musical notation has differed vastly over time – but has been adopted all over the globe. The modern musical notation we use today originated in European classical music, but is now used by musicians of many different genres throughout the world. The system, like that developed in France uses a five-line staff, and pitch is shown by placement of **notes** on the staff (sometimes modified by **accidentals**), and duration is shown with different **note values** and additional symbols such as **dots** and **ties**. There are also some specialised notation conventions, for example for percussion instruments or chord charts which contain little or no melodic information at all but provide detailed harmonic and rhythmic information, using slash notation and rhythmic notation. This is the most common kind of written music used by professional session musicians playing **jazz** or other forms of **popular music** and is intended primarily for the **rhythm section** (usually containing **piano**, **guitar**, **bass** and **drums**). We hope the reader is inspired by this book to find out more about this fascinating subject.

TO THE READER

THE following pages contain the substance of a course of ten lectures which I was privileged to deliver at Glasgow University in January and February 1927, as Cramb Lecturer for that session. The written word necessarily differs considerably from that which was spoken, and in the process of writing the lectures for publication I have purposely altered many details. The last one has been completely remodelled, because the local Press reports of it convinced me that I had not made my points clearly.

The syllabus of the course bore the clumsy title, 'Some aspects of Vocal Music, especially with regard to the setting of the English language in song, both choral and solo'. I was drawn to the subject because there were things which I wanted to say about Henry Purcell. The rest is grouped round a study of his work.

The course was illustrated at Glasgow by a series of vocal illustrations excellently sung by a number of Scottish musicians, both professional and amateur. Their names and what they sang are printed on another page. I wish to thank them and Mr. F. H. Bisset, to whose good offices I owed their collaboration, for all the trouble they took and the pleasure they gave. The memory of their singing has enlivened the task of writing and given me cause to endorse once more

Purcell's judgement, and to declare with him that music 'after all the learned Encomions [*sic*] that words can contrive, commends itself best by the performances of a skilful hand and an angelical voice'.

H. C. COLLES.

CRASTONS ORCHARD,
  YATTENDON,
    25 *August*, 1927.

CONTENTS

I.	The Nature of the Case	1
II.	The Emergence of the Vernacular	18
III.	'Stile Rappresentativo'	37
IV.	Towards English Opera	51
V.	Henry Purcell—Life and Times	69
VI.	Purcell to-day	86
VII.	Handel in London	103
VIII.	The Oratorio	121
IX.	The British Renaissance	135
X.	Open Questions	153

CRAMB LECTURES ILLUSTRATIONS
January to February 1927

I

'The Shepherd' (*soprano*) . . . . . Elgar
'Kind sir, you cannot have the heart' ('Gondoliers')
    (*soprano*) . . . . Sullivan
'Linden Lea' (*baritone*) . . . . Vaughan Williams
'Fear no more the heat o' the sun' (*baritone*) . . Walford Davies
'Sea Fever' (*baritone*) . . . . . John Ireland

Soprano: Mrs. Froggatt
Baritone: Mr. Robert Watson

II

MADRIGALS:
'Il bianco e dolce cigno' . . . . Arcadelt
'Quand mon mari' . . . . Orlandus Lassus
'The Silver Swan' . . . . Orlando Gibbons
'Cease sorrows' . . . . . . Weelkes
'Down in a flow'ry vale' . . . . . Festa
'On the plains' . . . . . . Weelkes

The Glasgow Orpheus Choir
Conductor: Mr. Hugh S. Roberton

III

Recit. No. 2 from 'Phoebus and Pan' . . . . Bach
    Mr. Albert Froggatt (*baritone*) and Mr. Francis Harford (*bass*)
Recit. No. 2 from 'The Christmas Oratorio' . . . Bach
    Mr. Robert Rennie (*tenor*)
Recit. and Arioso from 'St. Matthew Passion' . . Bach
    Mr. Robert Rennie (*tenor*) and Mr. Francis Harford (*bass*)

Cramb Lectures Illustrations

Excerpt from 'Parsifal' . . . . . . Wagner
    Mr. Francis Harford (*bass*)
Fragment from 'Orfeo' . . . . . Monteverdi
    Messenger (*soprano*): Mrs. Froggatt
    Shepherd (*tenor*): Mr. Robert Rennie
    Orpheus (*baritone*): Mr. Albert Froggatt

IV

'Dear, if you change' (*baritone*) . . . Dowland
'Sabrina fair' ('Comus'), (*baritone*) . . . Henry Lawes
'Nature's Song' ('Cupid and Death'), (*soprano and baritone*)   Locke
    Soprano: Mrs. Froggatt
    Baritone: Mr. Froggatt

V

Act II of 'Dido and Aeneas' and 'Dido's lament' (*soprano*)   Purcell
    The Stirling Choral Society
    Conductor: Mr. H. G. Barrett
    Soprano: Miss Margaret Barrett
    Tenor: Mr. Edmund Greig

VI

Bass solo, 'O Lord', trio, and 'Alleluia' chorus from Anthem, 'It is a good thing' . . . . . . Purcell
Alto solo, ''Tis Nature's Voice', and chorus, 'Soul of the World' from 'Ode on St. Cecilia's Day' . . . . Purcell
    The Glasgow Orpheus Choir
    Conductor: Mr. Hugh S. Roberton
    Bass: Mr. James Sellars
    Contralto: Miss Margaret Ferguson

VII

Tenor solo and chorus, 'Come if you dare' ('King Arthur')   Purcell
Tenor solo and chorus, 'The Trumpets' loud clangour' ('Ode on St. Cecilia's Day')   .   .   .   .   . Handel
Tenor solos from 'L'Allegro'   .   .   .   .   . Handel
      (*a*) 'Let me wander'
      (*b*) 'Straight mine eyes'
      The Glasgow Bach Choir
      Conductor: Mr. David T. Yacamini
      Tenor: Mr. Percy Manchester

VIII

Selection from 'Saul'   .   .   .   .   . Handel
      The Glasgow Bach Choir
      Conductor: Mr. David T. Yacamini
      Soprano: Miss Nellie Gordon
      Tenor: Mr. Percy Manchester

IX

Baritone solo, 'Then I looked', and chorus, 'To everything there is a season' from 'Beyond these voices'   .   .   . Parry
Soprano solo, 'Sometime walking' ('L'Allegro')   .   . Parry
Baritone solo, 'Cuttin' rushes'   .   .   .   .   . Stanford
Part-song, 'Heraclitus'   .   .   .   .   . Stanford
      The Glasgow Orpheus Choir
      Conductor: Mr. Hugh S. Roberton
      Soprano: Miss Janet Battersby
      Baritone: Mr. Albert Froggatt

X

Songs from Cycle for Tenor, 'On Wenlock Edge'   Vaughan Williams
        (*a*) 'Bredon Hill'
        (*b*) 'Is my team ploughing'
Part-song, 'Corpus Christi'   .   .   .   .   Peter Warlock
Madrigal, 'Flow, O my tears'   .   .   .   .   John Benet
Madrigal, 'All creatures now are merry minded'   .   John Benet

The Glasgow Orpheus Choir
Conductor: Mr. Hugh S. Roberton
Tenor: Mr. David T. Yacamini

CHAPTER I
THE NATURE OF THE CASE

'THE human pulse', said Zarlino, 'is the measure of the beats in music.' Zarlino was a great theorist of the sixteenth century, and, like others of his kind, he could occasionally light on a truism which all might understand in the midst of a maze of science intelligible only to the learned. Literally this means what the schoolgirl finds to her cost when she gets up to play her piece at the breaking-up concert. As her pulse quickens so does her music, till she breaks down at that awkward passage just before the *coda*.

But Zarlino touched on a larger truth than this. The human mechanism is responsible for more in music than its first element of a beating time. The basis of music in human physiology has not been very thoroughly explored, and it is far from my purpose to attempt an exploration for which I am not qualified; but the existence of that basis is evident enough. The human voice is the natural musical instrument and it orders all our ideas of pitch as the heart-beat decides those of time.

Why do we talk of the high C and the low C? The scientist tells us that the one is a note produced by double the number of vibrations per second which produce the other, but we are not aware of the vibrations; we do not count them. The pianist knows that one is to the right, the other to the left of his keyboard, but he does not adopt the language of politics and talk of the extreme right and the extreme left; he too thinks of the C's as high and low. His notions of music do not come through his keyboard; on the contrary, his keyboard is an approximation to his notions of music which are vocal. The singing-teacher talks of 'head register' and 'chest register' and the accuracy of his classification may be questioned, but we all know that it corresponds to something which happens when we sing the high C or the low C. One seems to come from the head, the other from the chest, and we say that the man who achieves the lowest C humanly possible is singing 'down in his boots'.

A clever young music student once suggested to me that it would be more reasonable to call a note of few vibrations a high one and one of many vibrations a low one on the analogy of the pyramid, thus:

Perhaps it would be, but it is not natural; it does not correspond to the action of the voice, and therefore we shall not do it. That is the trouble with clever people who apply reasoned ideas to music. They forget the difference between sound and music. The science of acoustics explains the former; the latter is the outcome of human feeling expressed primarily through certain actions of the body. Its base is in human nature. Cut it off from its base and it becomes merely a jingle of arbitrarily arranged sounds, which is what some modern composers are making of it.

Not only the general idea of high and low in music, but the scale, which carries out that idea in detail, is the outcome of vocal instinct selecting from the innumerable facts of sound which science offers as material for music.

Why do we think of four-part harmony as the normal arrangement, though common chords (the foundation of harmony) contain only three different notes? Three-part harmony would be more reasonable, but it would not answer to human requirements. The voices of men and women are pitched roughly an octave apart and each sex exhibits a high voice and a low voice differing in range by about half an octave (the interval of a fourth or fifth). In four-part harmony every one can join with comfort.

Why, to put the same question more broadly, do we

The Nature of the Case

think of harmony as one of the essentials of music, when all other civilizations of the world outside of Christian Europe have been content with melody, though some of their systems have been much more highly developed along their own melodic lines than our own?

The answer may be found in the fourteenth verse of the first chapter of the Acts of the Apostles, where it is written, 'These all continued with one accord in prayer and supplication, with the women.' The Christian religion, which recognized that woman had a soul to be saved equally with man, produced community singing, and so the music of Christian Europe was founded on the natural relations of pitch between the voices of both sexes. Community singing produced harmony; harmony produced the major-minor key system. The sonata and the symphony (purely instrumental forms) are essentially the product of that key system. So it comes that the worship of the early Church, common to both sexes, was destined to make possible the symphonies of Beethoven and the music-dramas of Wagner.

The major premise of the argument to which I invite attention in the following pages is that music is not based on an elaborate theory worked out scientifically by experts, but on human impulses finding expression through the voice and answering to human needs which vary with circumstances; that instrumental music is merely an extension of vocal music. At whatever stage we take the European development of the art of music we find its composers incorporating in their instrumental music their experience of vocal music. Every one of the recognized instrumental forms exhibits the process, and it is not outgrown as the forms mature. Rather it sinks deeper as the purely instrumental characteristics grow stronger.

This fact can be readily traced in the familiar types of music for the keyboard instruments, ranging historically from the virginal of the Elizabethan era to the pianoforte of to-day. The collection known as the 'Fitzwilliam Virginal Book' consists principally of three types of pieces by various composers: airs (generally popular folk-songs) with variations, dances (Pavans and Galliards), and fantasies (often called 'In Nomine'). The vocal influences are as clearly marked in the dances and fantasies as in those which are admittedly founded on song melodies, and only a rather primitive use of rapid scale passages, such as lie conveniently under the fingers on the keys, distinguishes their texture from that of the madrigal or motet. The several parts behave like voices, and we find points of imitation gravitating towards the style which was to be perfected more than a hundred years later in the fugues of J. S. Bach.

When we turn to Bach's 'Well-tempered Clavier', acknowledged to be the high-water mark of the instrumental fugue, we find that the traces of vocal origin are as strong there as in the work of his primitive predecessors. The subjects themselves are all of vocal range, rarely more than the compass of an octave and almost invariably centring on the interval of the fourth or fifth as the definition of melodic contour.[1] The structure of each fugue is vocal from the exposition to the piling up of the *stretto*; its decoration alone is instrumental.

If we come a hundred years later still, to the piano music of those composers generally described as 'romantics', we find the vocal structure and the instrumental decoration still more closely fused. We think of Chopin as essentially an instrumental composer. He was a pianist who wrote almost exclusively for his own instrument. Yet to play through the Nocturnes is to realize that every one is a song melody, an extended aria, a glorification of the manners of Italian opera particularly as exemplified in the style of Bellini. Take the Nocturne in B major (Op. 32, No. 1), for example, with its decorated melody centred on the

---

[1] Cf. *The Scope of Music*, by P. C. Buck, p. 34.

The Nature of the Case

rising fifth as surely as the fugue-subject of Bach here placed beside it.

Bach's development of his theme is that of choral music, Chopin's that of solo song, but the vocal principle is equally strong in both, and in this particular case of Chopin it is carried to the point of a final cadenza, aria-wise, and even to a suggestion of dramatic recitative when the aria is finished.

As with the composition of music itself, so with the making of instruments; it has been the ideal of musicians in all ages to provide themselves with instruments capable of doing what the human voice does. Those which achieve it successfully are recognized as the perfect instruments, and instruments are graded in estimation according to their measure of success in this respect. We call the violin family, together forming the string quartet, perfect, because they are capable of infinite gradations of pitch, the *portamento* between two notes of the scale, the just intonation of major and minor tones and semitones, which are natural to the voice, and which no instruments of fixed pitch, such as the pianoforte or the organ, can produce.

The organ and other wind instruments share with the strings the capacity for sustaining tone which belongs to the voice, but the organ falls below the strings and below the wind instruments blown by human breath, because it cannot vary the volume (play loud and soft) while it sustains. It is not susceptible to *nuance* except in so far as a 'swell' mechanism makes up for the deficiency.

The keyboard stringed instruments, having a string to a note, are, like the organ, all instruments of fixed intonation, and are also all inferior in sustaining power. The harpsichord, in which the strings are plucked by a mechanism, is, moreover, very little susceptible to *nuance*. It, therefore, is the instrument farthest removed from the vocal standard, and it was superseded by the pianoforte because the strings struck with hammers were found to produce a more sustained tone and the hammer mechanism gave the player a greater command of *nuance* than was obtainable from the plucked strings of the harpsichord.

Quite recently there has been a revival of the harpsichord; several brilliant performers on it have attracted attention, and a few composers have begun to write for it in preference to the pianoforte. The revival, in so far as it represents an attempt to reproduce the music of the past in its own conditions, is valuable both aesthetically and historically; in so far as it represents the desire of composers to turn their backs on the vocal standards of all music it is a symptom of decadence.

Music is often spoken of as a language. My contention is that the vocabulary, the grammar, and the syntax of that language have been brought into being by the expression of human feeling through the human voice; that, strictly speaking, there is no such thing as pure instrumental music, since instrumental sounds only become intelligible and sensible when they refer the mind of the participant to vocal experience of some sort.

At the present day there is a desire among certain composers to break with the vocal language. They are trying to make music independent of vocal associations. They would scrap the key system in favour of 'atonality', invent new scales and intervals, think in the

The Nature of the Case

equal temperament of the keyboard, dividing the octave up arithmetically. They claim to be inventing a new musical language and their experiments are interesting. They have only to go on talking their new language long enough to discover whether other people can enter into it, understand it, and talk it with them. At present it must be regarded as a musical equivalent to Esperanto, the universal tongue which nobody talks.

We are reminded that all the innovations of great artists have been spurned in their own generation because the ordinary mind required time to grow up to them. The ordinary mind certainly required a little time to discover that the whole of Wagner's music-dramas were based on vocal principles already in themselves familiar from long association. That is a very different thing from inviting the ordinary mind to strip itself of these associations and begin again on a new basis devised by some theorist, and the response of the ordinary mind to such an invitation can be foreseen by any one except a theoretic musician.

We need not consider the excrescences of modern composers at this stage. A further word may be devoted to them later. It is time to introduce the minor premise of the argument, which will require less explanation than the major one. It is simply that song depends for its existence on words as well as music, and that it is as natural to mankind to sing words as to speak them.

Thomas Morley in a famous work[1] of instruction and criticism made a simple division of the art into music made 'on a ditty' and music made without a ditty. The division was not quite the same as that between vocal and instrumental music, because Morley recognized the prevalent, but artificial, practice of his time of singing without words. He saw, however, that the art of setting words to music, that is composing to a ditty or text of any sort, was something different from

[1] *Plaine and Easie Introduction to Practicall Musick*, 1597.

other musical composition. The words must to a certain extent condition the style of the music, must hold the composer in check. Indeed, Morley specially extolled the instrumental fantasy as that in which the composer is held by nothing and therefore may display his musicianship most fully and indulge in every flight of fancy that occurs to him. The union of words and music was nevertheless to Morley a serious and a complicated problem, because, as I shall try to show in the next chapter, it had been brought before him and his Elizabethan contemporaries in a new and vivid way. It is only at a fairly advanced stage of artistic evolution that music begins to stand alone, to be made (as we say) for its own sake.

Among primitive peoples singing always goes with words or actions, and frequently with both. Songs are not made up by them solely as tunes but as a means of doing something else. The tunes help the singer to memorize words or to give expression to feelings prompted by words. Or they are allied to actions of some sort, such as dancing or carrying on more or less mechanical occupations. Mr. Cecil Sharp[1] drew attention to the impossibility of getting the traditional folk-singers who had learnt their music aurally to repeat words or music separately. To such singers, song, words and music, is a single concept practically incapable of analysis into its parts. A very slight acquaintance with folk-song of any sort will enable you to recall that the folk-singer only abandons words when the song is to accompany some action such as the hauling of the capstan shanties, or the 'wauking' songs, and other songs of occupation which Mrs. Kennedy Fraser collected in the Hebrides. Even where words with a sense of their own are abandoned, because the action or the dance supplies its own sense, the natural singer falls back on some syllabic jingle in conjunction with the tune, such as the 'Heave ho' or the 'Ranzo' of the shanties. He needs

[1] *English Folk-song: Some Conclusions*, by C. J. Sharp, 1907.

The Nature of the Case 9

something of a verbal description to vocalize with, or to define rhythm. The 'fa-la-la' refrains of the dancing songs of Thomas Morley himself give a sophisticated instance of this, from which we may draw the deduction that words, or at any rate vowel-sounds separated from one another by consonants, are the most natural means of phrasing with the voice. Let any one try to sing the following on a vowel-sound alone, 'oh' or 'ah', and that point will be fully established.

With a fa la la, la, la, la la la la la.

We may take it then that the alliance of music with words of some sort to make song is the natural habit of mankind arising out of the structure of the vocal organs, and that it is only by an effort of virtuosity that mankind can arrive at singing without the aid of words.

That is possibly the reason why modern choirs and their conductors are so fond of those tortuous 'um-ings' and 'ah-ings' that modern composers so obligingly write for them. They feel as clever as the performing bear who has learnt to stand on his hind-legs; they also make the listener feel as uncomfortable as the bear looks. Such efforts, whether we regard them as flights of genius or as momentary aberrations of sense, are evidently exceptional. They do not impugn the general truth of the saying: No words, no song, to which I have already suggested may be added: No song, no developed art of music.

The making of a song, then, presents a dual problem. We cannot judge a song to be good or bad solely on the strength or weakness of its musical qualities. The good song, whether a simple folk-tune or an elaborate aria, is one which heightens through the music what the words have to say, the music giving them some sort of eloquence which they would not have possessed without it.

I saw it stated in an article recently that Stravinsky 'sees no reason why an impression conveyed in one art should be merely duplicated in another. A fine poem to him gains nothing by being set to music, and this explains how in his later works he came to choose words which in themselves possess no beauty and very little sense'.[1]

If this is a true presentation of Stravinsky's aesthetic views, it explains more than the writer claims. It explains why a man of undeniable genius has fallen into writing music which possesses no beauty and very little sense. In his exclusive pursuit of Art he has lost hold of the plain facts of the case, and forgotten the natural in search of the obscure. It is natural to the singer to think of what the words say and to express his feeling about them in music. It is unnatural to him to talk nonsense and think music simultaneously. The effort to do so is liable to result in a duplicated nonsense.

Wagner spoke of music as being fertilized by poetry. That is to regard the matter from the point of view of a composer whose brain is teeming with music which only takes form by the touch of a poetic suggestion. The listener to a song will often feel that the reverse is the case; for the great masters from Purcell to Brahms, including Wagner himself (who set his own words), have frequently by their music given the poetic suggestion to words which hardly seemed to contain it in themselves. Whichever is the fertilizer in each particular case, Milton touched the truth of the matter when he invoked Voice and Verse to

> Wed your divine sounds and mix'd power employ
> Dead things with inbreathed sense able to pierce.

In the practical process of composition the words generally come first. Something gleaned from them provides the impulse which creates desire in the composer to turn that particular text into song by the

[1] *Grove's Dictionary of Music and Musicians*, Edition III, article 'Stravinsky'.

exercise of his art. The first thing he does is to steep himself in the words so that his mind becomes possessed by their mood. That process may be quick or slow. Schumann said of Schubert that everything he touched turned into music, and the story of Schubert coming across the translation of Shakespeare's 'Hark, hark, the lark', and instantly writing the song on the back of the restaurant menu, shows the case of a man so responsive to the impulse of words that the steeping process was practically instantaneous. Mr. Ernest Newman[1] has discussed this process illuminatingly, and, describing the composer as falling into a state of clairvoyance, has shown that the state may occur too rapidly and cause him to write too soon. This means that he may be seized with an idea, possibly a subsidiary one, in the poem, or be captivated by a phrase, so that the whole of his music is made relative to that idea or phrase. The result in such a case is no complete presentation of the poetic suggestion in music at all, but at best only a partially successful song.

Let us consider the matter with reference to one kind of song, the setting of the short lyrical poem, by which I mean a poem which does not, like the ballad, tell a story, or, like the scena, portray a dramatic situation, or, like the epic, dwell contemplatively on great events. The lyric poem just catches a mood, and, as it were, crystallizes it in verse; its mood can generally be characterized by a single word such as love, joy, peace, sorrow, yearning, or fatalism.

As illustrations of the type I purposely avoid here the masterpieces of classical song and choose rather specimens of English poems set to music by the good rather than the great among composers. In choosing the songs of four living Englishmen I attempt no comparison of their capacities as composers, but only an examination of their approach to the several poems they choose. Each has had to decide what there is in

[1] *Hugo Wolf*, p. 182, note 1.

the mood of the poem which he wishes his music to amplify, and how far to fasten attention on the main mood to the exclusion of subsidiary ones, which may either contribute to it or detract from its force. Even the short lyric may contain innumerable side-currents of thought and feeling which offer dangerous pitfalls to the composer. By ignoring them his song may become merely a superficial rendering of the poem; by following them too readily he may lose his musical thread. The composer requires extraordinary suppleness of mind to be sufficiently sensitive to the poet's imagery without losing hold of his own musical design.

The first example is Vaughan Williams's setting of William Barnes's 'On Linden Lea'. The essence[1] of the poem lies in the last four lines:

> I be free to go abroade
> Or take again my homeward road
> To where for me the apple tree
> Do lean down low on Linden Lea.

It is the song of a countryman free from the trammels of responsibility and the cares of ambition. He does not think much about even the apple tree on Linden Lea. He did not put it there, probably he does not even prune it. He does not argue about why its leaning lines appeal to him, but it does give him a sense of well-being to see it there. He goes abroad and takes his homeward road over and over again. He does not want to do anything else.

This mood is so all-pervading that the composer will not risk disturbing it by varying the details of the tune even when the thought turns from the poet's own rural content to the townsfolk who 'make money faster'. The song is 'strophic', that is with the same music to each verse, like a folk-song. Any other musical treatment would have been liable to introduce a subtlety

---

[1] Mr. H. P. Greene has pointed out that practically every song poem of this type contains what he calls a 'masterphrase'. See *Interpretation in Song*, p. 17.

The Nature of the Case 13

beyond the experience of the supposed singer. One would not say this could not be done, because there are instances where a stroke of genius refutes dogmatism, but we can see that the composer was fully justified in not attempting to go beyond the expression of the placid mood, which has suggested to him a tune as spontaneous in curve as the leaning branch of the apple tree itself.

It is worth while to place beside this Walford Davies's setting of Shakespeare's 'Fear no more the heat o' the Sun' (*Cymbeline*). Here the prevailing mood is something quite different, but it is no less all-pervading. Death is a stark certainty, and life marches towards it in a grim procession. Only when it is reached it brings 'quiet consummation'; there is then nothing to fear, and pity is futile. Clearly the march of the music must be unbroken, yet to set the four stanzas alike would not do here. The matter is too serious. Some note must be taken of the several images used to enforce the implacable mood set in the opening intonation.

Note the subtle changes of harmony and melody used to give weight to the conclusion without breaking the march rhythm.

I would draw particular attention to this song, partly because it is very little known and partly because the clear-eyed acceptance of fate without self-persuasion or personal sentiment about it which belongs to Shakespeare's lines has found a counterpart in the direct unswerving lines of the melody. Save for this coda, the song is almost hard in tone.

The third instance is that of a song in which I venture to think that the composer has only half caught the mood. Possibly he has seized too quickly at a single aspect of it. John Ireland's popular setting of Masefield's 'Sea Fever' certainly reflects something of the man's yearning desire; but do you feel that the composer has actually entered into the seafaring man's point of view in the way in which Vaughan Williams has identified himself with the Dorset Farmer or Walford Davies has risen to the Shakespearian apostrophe of Death? There is a plaintiveness, almost a whine, about the melody and the harmony which to me suggests the landsman contemplating a rough channel passage rather than the seaman to whom battle with the elements is the breath of life. The defect is not in the construction. The form of the melody keeps as close to the form of the verse as does that of 'Linden Lea', nor has the composer missed any direct implication of the words. Yet his song is like a poem read in the wrong tone of voice, as the clerical reader who reads the Bible in church with intelligence and due accentuation and punctuation too often reads. The effect is enervating where it should be stimulating.

The instance suggests that seizing a mood implies giving the right lilt to the words through the rhythmic movement of the music, and this leads me to make a preliminary examination of the technical difficulty of accommodating poetic metre to musical time, a point with which we shall be more fully concerned later. An illustration away from the songs before us may serve to make that clear. Milton praised Henry Lawes for

The Nature of the Case 15

catching the right lilt of his lines in a sonnet which begins

> Harry, whose tuneful and well-measured song,
> First taught our English music how to span
> Words with just note and accent;

If we take this trochaic metre of five feet and express it in five musical bars of long and short (making the bar correspond with the foot) we get this:

[musical notation in 3/8 time]

Obviously, to set Milton's words in this rhythm would be fatal; quite apart from the excessive accent thrown on 'and' we get a monotonous emphasis of the metre of the kind popularly described as 'sing-song', which is the very opposite of 'just note and accent'. If, on the other hand, we try to sing at the time of speech while keeping the 3/8 time we get something like the following:

[musical notation]
Har-ry, whose tune-ful and well-mea-sured song

[musical notation]
First taught our En-glish mu-sic how to span

[musical notation]
Words with just note and ac-cent [not to scan]

The bars no longer correspond to feet, for the five of the line are contracted into a four-bar phrase. Within that phrase are all sorts of smaller rhythms due to the attempt to reach the syllabic values of the words. You will realize also that a composer might, probably would, depart still further both from the poetic metre and the speech rhythm for purposes of musical expression, and could do so without any violence to the accentuation. The group of four quavers in a bar suggests, for example, a different time reading of the second line:

[musical notation in 2/4 time]
First taught our En-glish mu - sic . . . how to span.

There are then three concomitants, poetic metre, speech

rhythm, and musical time, which may be at variance and must be accommodated; they may be contestants but ought to be colleagues in the complete expression of words through music.

The fourth song of the group chosen, Elgar's 'The Shepherd', is put forward as a case where the composer has seized the mood of the poem successfully and has found the right lilt for the verse as far as the general conception is concerned, but has not let it work through to the details. You have only to hear the line which ends both verses 1 and 2,

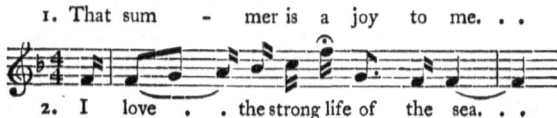

to perceive that he has not let the question of 'just note and accent' disturb him very seriously. His impulse is wrapped up in the free course of the tune; he will not check his impulse on any account. In this he is right, but in the perfect song he would not have to check it, because the tune would be supple enough to bend to the words without breaking.

If you want a simple song where the tune is no less self-existent than Elgar's and yet is swayed by every suggestion both of meaning and of accent supplied by the words, turn to Elsie's appeal to the Grand Inquisitor in the finale to the first act of *The Gondoliers*:

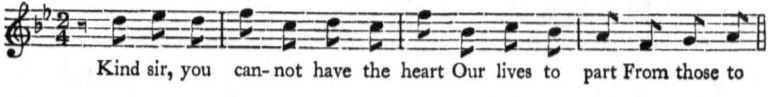

Throughout the musical phrases are balanced with an exquisite precision, while every inflexion of the tune serves to point without a hint of exaggeration the shy earnestness of the appellant. The audiences who

The Nature of the Case

chuckle over Gilbert's humour and guffaw at the leering grimaces of the Grand Inquisitor on the stage are little impressed by the subtleties of Sullivan's mastery over words and music displayed here and in a thousand passages of the Savoy Operas.

The intimate relationships between words and music, which we take for granted to such an extent that we only become conscious of them when we miss them, were only gradually appreciated by composers in the process of a long historical development. I propose to look into that development, especially in regard to the English language in song.

From what has been already said it will be recognized that the peculiarities of a language must deeply affect the characteristics of melody produced in contact with it. One might go further and say that the much canvassed question of nationalism in musical composition depends in the last resort on the associations between music and language. If Russian music differs from German music it is largely because the two languages differ fundamentally, and if English music is akin to German the reason is not so much to be found in some wilful homage paid by us to the alien as in the fact that the two languages have much in common.

I hope to show, however, that the English language, having characteristics of its own, some of which raise peculiar difficulties for the musician who deals honestly with them, has in fact produced an English melody.

CHAPTER II
THE EMERGENCE OF THE VERNACULAR

And the whole earth was of one language and one speech. . . . And they said, Go to, let us build us a city, and a tower whose top may reach unto heaven; and let us make us a name, lest we be scattered abroad upon the face of the whole earth. . . .
And the Lord said, Behold, the people is one and they have all one language, and this they begin to do. . . . Go to, let us go down and there confound their language, that they may not understand one another's speech. So the Lord scattered them abroad from thence upon the face of all the earth: and they left off to build the city. GENESIS xi. 1–8.

THIS description of the confounding of the peoples in the very act of consolidation is paralleled in many phases of history, but in none so closely as by what took place in Europe early in the sixteenth century. The whole of medieval civilization had been built upon and was knit together by a common language. Latin, the accepted tongue of the Western Church, was the means by which the learned of all countries were wont to communicate. Learning was the property of the Church, an international society which knew no frontiers; ecclesiastics held high legal offices and conducted diplomatic missions by its means. In an age when the speed of international communication was the pace of a horse and literature could only be disseminated in copies made by the hand of the scribe, the existence of scribes in all the monasteries of Western Europe, having command of a language intelligible among themselves, was a matter of great practical convenience to princes who were dependent on the learning of churchmen for the carrying on of government. The secular structure of Feudalism owed almost as much to the Latin language as did the unity and continuity of the Church herself, and so long as the Church could maintain the pre-eminence given her by her language the growing sense of nationalism could not reach the point of disruption of the European society.

The Emergence of the Vernacular

Music, regarded as one of the learned sciences, was no less subject to this dominance than the other arts. From the age of plainsong composition to the treatises on the 'Ars Nova', and thence again to the great choral schools which culminated in Palestrina, we find the musicians, like all other cultured folk, thinking in Latin. It is true that since to sing is a natural activity of mankind, like walking, talking, and making love (a fact which singing-teachers would do well to remember at the present day), there always was an intuitive and unpremeditated art of the people which joined melody with whatever language it was natural to them to use, and we get glimpses of that art occasionally in written records, sometimes influencing the art of the ecclesiastics or appropriating the ecclesiastical technique to its own ends. The English round of the thirteenth century, 'Sumer is icumen in', is the most famous instance of this. The French *chansons* and the Italian madrigals both had their existence long before that confounding of the common language and that scattering abroad which was the outcome of the Renaissance.

We are apt to think of the dispersal of the Latin Babel as a thing effected with dramatic suddenness by the religious changes of the sixteenth century called the Reformation, and that is a view natural especially to a Scottish audience, since, as Mr. G. M. Trevelyan says, 'England approached the Reformation through the Renaissance; Scotland approached the Renaissance through the Reformation.'[1] Of that more presently, when we come to our own special problem; at the moment I would merely remind you that it was the influence of the Renaissance in Italy which propagated vernacular poetry and stimulated the composition of choral songs to Italian words. There were two types of these: the *frottola*, or popular part-song, in which folk-tunes and familiar melodies were set to a simple har-

[1] *History of England*, by G. M. Trevelyan, p. 331: Longmans, Green & Co., 1926.

mony suitable for singing by more or less unlettered folk, often out of doors and in popular festivals of every kind, and the madrigal which from the first postulated a higher standard of culture in the composition of both words and music.

It was indeed through union with the poetic form of the madrigal that the art of music in its higher branches was to become un-Latinized. The madrigal offered a concise and manageable literary form to the musician, in contrast with the long narrative poems, romances, or ballads in which much of the vernacular literature of Europe before the Renaissance was developed. The madrigal was in fact just such a lyric as we were considering in the previous chapter in connexion with the composers of to-day, a poem of ten or a dozen lines long (it never had the strict form and measure of the sonnet), which expressed a single feeling or enshrined a single mood, and therefore offered to the musician something which he could make his own and carry over, as it were, from the words into the style of the music.

It is little wonder, then, that we find the composers in Italy (many of them were natives of other countries, notably the Netherlands and Spain) applying the art of vocal counterpoint acquired for the purposes of Latin church music to the task of a more direct verbal expression in the setting of madrigals. The Church and its language had evolved a certain kind of technique of musical composition exactly suited to its purpose. The authorities were always anxious to keep that technique within bounds, and the medieval history of the growth of the art is punctuated with records of complaints against the enterprise of composers and the improvisations of singers, who in various ways attempted what we now call 'self expression' in the music designed for church worship. The Church maintained a corporate and impersonal ideal; the artist is always an individualist; hence the conflict which continued from

The Emergence of the Vernacular

the edict of Pope John XXII (1322) to the Council of Trent (1545). Composers, disciplined to act in accordance with the corporate ideal in setting the official texts of the liturgy, found an outlet for personal feelings in the composition of the unofficial and wholly secular madrigal.

And yet to modern ears it often seems as though they hardly took full advantage of their opportunities, and that even those who poured out one set of madrigals after another did not venture very far away from the ecclesiastical style in their secular work. It is necessary to bear in mind that to the earlier madrigalists church music represented practically the whole art of music. Any different style had to be a more or less slow process of evolution, the result of a gradual experience. Also it may be suggested that to replace the Latin tongue with the Italian was a comparatively small change and one which did not instantly necessitate a complete change of front in the composer. The structure of the two languages being near of kin (Italian may be called the daughter of Latin), composers in many cases scarcely felt that they were attacking any new problem in passing from the one to the other.

We may take the well-known instance of Jacob Arcadelt's madrigal, 'Il bianco e dolce cigno,'[1] published in his first book of madrigals at Venice in 1539, as an instance of this. The poem contrasts the sad fate of the swan who dies singing with the blessed fate of the poet who finds content in death. Since death must end his sorrows he would face a thousand deaths to win so great a release. The words favour that reflective placidity of outline which is characteristic of the purest types of church music in the sixteenth century. There is little temptation to lay expressive emphasis on one phrase at the expense of another, and yet Arcadelt indulges in one point of quite direct verbal expression

[1] Book II, No. 1 of Barclay Squire's *Ausgewählte Madrigale*, Breitkopf and Härtel.

in the moment where the tears of the poet are contrasted by a chromatic harmony with the swan song:

Much more striking, however, is the emphasis which by wholly contrapuntal means the composer gives to the last line,

> Di mille mort' il di sarei contento.

He expends the whole of his musicianship in building a climax of exquisitely flowing fugal entries, and out of the interval of the rising fourth he achieves a consummate piece of art comparable to that of J. S. Bach himself (cf. p. 5.)

The two passages placed side by side give a concrete instance of the instrumental style of the eighteenth century springing straight from the vocal one of the sixteenth; for the moment we are more concerned to observe that the particular device is employed by Arcadelt in response to the call of the words for the endless wreathed phrases of fugue. We are apt to think of fugue as the strictest of closely calculated musical designs. In this instance we see it making its appearance for solely expressive ends.

Arcadelt was a representative member of that group of Netherlandish composers who gravitated to Italy as to the centre of the ecclesiastical civilization ostensibly to practise there the art of church music. He held an appointment as a church musician at St. Mark's in Venice, and it was there that no less than five books of his madrigals, each containing some forty numbers, were composed and published. We know little of him beyond the written record of his work, in which, however, we may discern an artist of high attainments, if not of the highest genius, pursuing an uninterrupted career in his adopted home just in that period when the Venetian republic had reached and was passing from the zenith of its political eminence, when the full force of the Roman Renaissance was making itself felt in its architecture and the richest period of its painting had culminated in Titian.

A very different career was that of Arcadelt's countryman Orlando di Lasso (Orlandus Lassus), of a younger generation, who, though his first book of Italian Madrigals (1555) was also published in Venice, led a life filled with the wider experience of men and affairs that travel and conversance with several nations, their manners and speech, may bring. Lasso was closely contemporary [1] with the famous Roman composer Palestrina, universally acknowledged to be the man who brought the sixteenth century church music to its highest development. Lasso as a composer of Latin church music was scarcely behind Palestrina, while in

[1] Lasso and Palestrina died in the same year, 1594.

secular work he outshone him. Lasso's early publication of works both in Venice and Antwerp show him even at the age of twenty-five or so to have possessed a reputation which bestrode Europe, and the ease with which he turns from sacred to secular, adapting his musical style to the particular task in hand, reveals the ready versatility of the man of the world.

Much of his working life was spent in the service of the Duke of Bavaria at Munich, for whom he wrote the famous 'Penitential Psalms', but we hear of him later visiting both Paris and Italy again. There is a legend, not substantiated, that he paid a visit to England. The important point for us is that besides the Latin church music he made choral songs of various types in three languages, Italian, French, and German, and in each showed a subtle perception of the qualities of the language.

The little example of Lasso chosen here for illustration shows him in his lightest vein. It is from a set of French *chansons* for four voices, published in Antwerp in 1564, about the middle of his life. The poem 'Quand mon mari'[1] is a little character study of a young woman who suffers under the hand of a wife-beating husband. When he comes in he is sure to beat her over the head with the soup ladle. She is in terror of her life; he is a nasty, jealous brute, and the reason is (she gloats *sotto voce* over the reason) 'I am young and he is old'. The subject is not edifying, and the poem is not beautiful; I choose it to show how far Lasso could get away from the classical, statuesque manner of the madrigal as represented by the example of Arcadelt. His treatment of it in music is certainly as vividly human as is possible when four voices (S. A. T. B.) have to distribute the sentiments of one young woman between them. The energetic accentuation of the epithets *rioteux*, *grommeleux*, suggests that her tongue can return the blows of the soup ladle with stinging

[1] Book II, No. 6 of Barclay Squire's *Ausgewählte Madrigale*.

The Emergence of the Vernacular

interest, and in the repetitions of the last phrase she is evidently hugging to herself the comforting assurance of her capacity to outlive her tormentor.

These slight samples, particularly the last, must serve as evidence of how far the choral style was capable of extension from its primary purpose of church worship, and how, under the influence of the lyric, composers of the mid-sixteenth century had discovered the possibility of both seizing a mood and reflecting the lilt of words in their musical rhythms.

When we come to consider our special problem of the English language in song we may be inclined to doubt Mr. Trevelyan's dictum, quoted above, so far as England herself was concerned. I have suggested that on the Continent the emergence of the vernacular was one of the effects of the Renaissance. In England the madrigal and its attendant forms of choral secular song hardly made their appearance until the ecclesiastical Reformation had become an accomplished fact in the reign of Elizabeth, and undoubtedly the spur given to composers to treat the English language seriously in song was the order to sing the church service in English and the publication in 1549 of the first *Book of Common Prayer*. Mr. Trevelyan, however, is dealing with the broad aspects of history, and we are here concerned with only one of its minor manifestations. The intellectual conceptions propagated by the Renaissance led up to the decision in favour of an English liturgy, a thing which in itself by no means implied a change of religion from Catholicism to Protestantism. The claim of continuity was maintained, and, indeed, the book itself was soon found to be far too Catholic in its principles and in the rites and ceremonies it enjoined to satisfy the Protestant party, which gathered strength during the reign of Edward VI. The main struggles of the Reformation, the theological controversies, the persecutions and counter-persecutions, were still all to come. The first Prayer Book was merely their harbinger; it asserted the right of the Church in England to institute local reform and establish local uses many of which were already prevalent without authority. It is typical of English habits that the change was made without any official guidance as to how its enactments as regards singing should be carried out.[1]

When Martin Luther a quarter of a century earlier had determined on a German Mass and a German Psalm-book he called Johann Walther into consultation, to work out a scheme for the contribution of music to his new form of worship. Walther brought the expert knowledge of a musician to bear on the amateur suggestions of Luther, who was just enough of a practical musician to try over on a flute the tunes which came up for discussion. Thus foundations of a Lutheran Church Music were laid which were in process of time to have a world-wide influence in the German chorale. Exactly two hundred years after Luther had picked out tunes on his flute J. S. Bach produced the *Johannes Passion*; the grain of seed had become the mightiest of trees.

[1] Similarly in 1927 a new version of the *Book of Common Prayer* was put forward which proposed important alterations in words sung for three hundred years to traditional music without apparently any consideration of the musical adaptation necessary, e.g. 'Because there is none other that ruleth the world but only Thou, O God'.

The Emergence of the Vernacular

England had no such forcible direction as the almost papal decrees of Luther gave to German church musicians. Archbishop Cranmer, who was responsible for the first Prayer Book, had indeed a general idea that its music should be simple, and to this idea he had given expression rather earlier, when he proposed to Henry VIII that a safe canon of taste would be that of one note to a syllable.[1] It was an inadequate suggestion which incidentally showed the author's ignorance of the nature of the act of song, but it offered a rough working principle, something which the practical musician could take as a starting-point in the bewildering work of adaptation which the change of language made necessary.

Every choirmaster will readily imagine the chaos which must have existed on Whitsunday 1549, when priests and choirs, armed only with their old service books and knowing only the traditions of the Latin Office, tried for the first time to sing the Ordinary of the Mass in English.[2] The result must have been something very different from the Pentecostal intention of allowing men to hear in their own tongue the wonderful works of God.

Order was brought out of chaos, however, shortly after by the agency of a man who had special qualifications for the task. John Merbecke was a singing man and organist in 'His Majesty's Free Chapel of St. George in Windsor Castle'. He was known for a tiresome fellow in the reign of Henry VIII, when the first changes in the Church were impending, because he would not mind his own business but concerned himself with theology. He was in fact arrested for heresy

[1] This suggestion, contained in a private letter, has often been referred to as though it were a rule of the reformers having practically the force of law. It was nothing of the sort. Cranmer merely voiced a prevalent desire for simplification in music which the Catholic Church of the Continent shared with that in England.

[2] English settings of parts of the Liturgy had in fact been composed and presumably used, but they cannot have been generally available.

and condemned (26 July 1541), but was saved from the extreme penalty by the intervention of one of his judges, Bishop Gardiner of Winchester, who apparently talked to him kindly and tried to persuade him not to interfere in matters which he did not understand. Merbecke explained that he was compiling a Concordance of the English Bible, and showed his interlocutors how such a work might be used. They probably came to the conclusion that his Biblical studies were harmless if not very profitable. At any rate he was sent back to his post at St. George's; when the open Bible was accepted as a principle of religion, he was able to publish his Concordance with a dedication to Edward VI, and he retained the emoluments of his post at St. George's throughout the Marian reaction and under the Elizabethan settlement until his death in 1585.

His experience as a church singer and his studies in the purest source of English literature exactly fitted him to supply what was so sorely needed, a plain chant for the new English service book, and this he did in *The Booke of Common Praier Noted* (1550). That book has received such an accession of importance in connexion with the modern Catholic revival in the English Church, it has been so widely canvassed and so completely misunderstood, that it will be worth while here to consider in a few words what it was that Merbecke aimed at doing. On its musical side it is a mere *pasticcio* of familiar plain-song melodies (the psalm tones, the Ambrosian Te Deum, the Missa pro defunctis,[1] &c., simplified and, from the scholar's point

[1] Sir Richard Terry analysed the sources of Merbecke's melody in a paper read before the Musical Association (see *Proceedings*, 1918–19). He pointed out that Merbecke's musical method followed 'a practice common enough on the Continent, as exhibited in the well-known "Missa Regia" and the Masses of Dumont and others'. Terry, however, completely missed the meaning of Merbecke's method of dealing with the words, and fell into an error perhaps excusable in one whose personal experience had been confined to the Latin Office.

The Emergence of the Vernacular

of view, debased) with a certain amount of originally invented melody in a style agreeable to that of plainsong.

In order to express the syllabic values and accents of the English language the more truly, however, Merbecke adopted a special notation, which he explained carefully in a short preface at the beginning of the book. The black-headed notes which he used on a four-lined stave look at first sight like plain-song, but they have three main values which may be described as long, ordinary, and short. To these he added modifications, a note with a pause mark over it, that is, a sign to show the end of a sentence or clause, and a dot (prycke) to lengthen the ordinary note by one-half its value as in modern music. To the three chief notes he gave names according to their shapes and explained that they corresponded to the three chief notes of mensural music (breve, semibreve, and minim). Setting out his explanation in tabular form we get

1. 'Strene' (i.e. stretched like a banner between two poles)   Breve
2. 'Square'   Semibreve
3. 'Pycke' (i.e. pike-head or diamond shape)   Minim
4. Close (only to be used at the end of a verse)

This is straightforward enough, but modern editors have misread it simply because they could not believe that Merbecke was as clear-sighted as he actually was. Some have thought that he used the black-headed notes in order to produce a pseudo-archaic effect to the eye, that it was in fact a piece of Wardour Street musicmongering. They have further taken 'pycke' to be a misprint for 'prycke', and so mixed up the shortest note with the dot. One school of thought or thoughtlessness has declared that he meant to write English plain-song, i.e. music without any measure of notes;

another has declared that his use of these different values meant a strict time measure. Both are equally wrong on Merbecke's own showing, and they have gone wrong because they have thought of it as a book more than three hundred years old in which there was bound to be some quaintness, instead of visualizing the practical situation Merbecke wanted to meet. He was a modern-minded man with no love for outworn ecclesiastical conventions. He would have been the last person to revert to an old-fashioned notation for the sake of appearances. The fact was that the ordinary notation of mensural music in which he had written his own Latin Mass for five voices would not serve (it was too elaborate), and the old notation of plain-song was inadequate because it would not help the singer to accentuate the English language properly. He therefore fell back on a cross between the two, using just so much of each as would be practically helpful. Though the notes were to be long, ordinary, and short, they were not to represent a strictly counted out measure in proportion of 1 : 2. Wherever the syllables of the words would naturally stress themselves aright in the singing, Merbecke used only the square (ordinary) notes, for example:

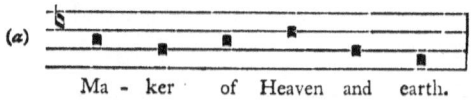

(a) Ma - ker of Heaven and earth.

which modern choirs, aided by modern editors, almost invariably contract into

(b) Ma - ker of Heaven and earth.

with a horrible jigging effect. On the other hand, wherever the group of syllables represented some nicety of the English language (especially in connexion with a word derived from Latin, and therefore particularly dangerous to the singer accustomed to Latin) he

The Emergence of the Vernacular

wrote out the group, using his resources of short notes or dots as occasion served, for example:

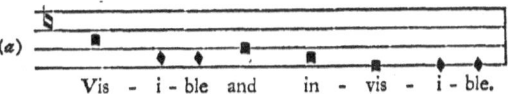

Here the association with 'visibilium' required a safeguard, yet choirs and editors to-day turn the cadence into

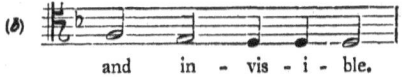

Merbecke's choice of words to receive treatment in measured music shows always the experience of the singer. He was no theorist and he produced no system. *The Booke of Common Praier Noted* was merely a practical guide probably produced hurriedly to meet an emergency, and actually a first essay in accommodating the prose rhythms of the language to a free musical rhythm. That is why it holds a unique place in the history of English song. Its actual use in its own day was short-lived, for the first Prayer Book was superseded by the second in 1552, and neither Merbecke nor any one else took the trouble to adapt the notes to the wording of the second book, but it remains for us as evidence that at least one musician in the middle of the sixteenth century had realized the special problems which the English language presents in song, and had sought and to a certain extent found a solution of them.

We are all familiar with the parrot-cry, 'English is so bad for singing'. It is repeated over and over by people who have heard *Aïda* or *La Bohème* sung in Italian by Italian singers and have then heard those popular operas translated into bad English and sung by singers trained by foreign methods to disregard the characteristics of their own language as much as possible. English has its difficulties, and its difficulties when they are well handled make its chief beauties in song. The variety of its vowel-sounds (e.g. 'All we like sheep have gone astray', seven vowel-sounds in eight syllables and four of them on 'a'), its conglomerations of consonants (as in 'strength'), its syllables without any fully vocalized vowel at all (as the last of 'visible'), are generally recognized as characteristics to be specially dealt with by both composers and singers. Comparatively few have recognized the existence of the syllabic groups which can bring an infinite variety of subsidiary rhythms into a melody set to English words whether poetry or prose. John Merbecke was the first to do so; his *Booke of Common Praier Noted* was a preliminary reconnaissance of the language for the purposes of song, and it was made almost a generation before the madrigal of the Italian Renaissance began to exert an active influence on English composers.

The story of how the madrigal fashion was set by that great master ('never to be named without reverence', as Thomas Morley says), William Byrd, is too well known to require recapitulation here. Byrd, in the very year of the defeat of the Spanish Armada (1588), published his first book called *Psalms, Songs, and Sonnets of Sadness and Piety*, &c., and the publication was the signal for an outpouring from the press of similar collections of secular choral songs by so many hands that for once in our history it really seems that England possessed something which could be called a 'School' of composers. Dr. E. H. Fellowes[1] has in our own generation placed the whole product of that school in the hands of the modern musician, and has taken away all excuse for ignorance of their achieve-

---

[1] *The English Madrigal School* (36 vols.), edited by E. H. Fellowes, published by Stainer and Bell, contains Madrigal publications by twenty-four composers: Morley, Gibbons, Wilbye, Farmer, Weelkes, Byrd, Lichfield, Tomkins, Ward, Farnaby, Bateson, Benet, Kirbye, Pilkington, Carlton, Youll, East, Alison, Vautor, R. Jones, Mundy, Cavendish, Greaves, Holborne.

The Emergence of the Vernacular

ments. The existence of such a school, although it flourished after the ecclesiastical Reformation had been accomplished, is evidence of the truth of Mr. Trevelyan's statement about England's approach to the Reformation through the Renaissance. No parallel movement of the kind is found in Scotland. Further quotation from the same source will shed light on the difference:

'If the year 1559 is to count as the first of modern England, it is still more decisively the birth year of modern Scotland. The precise coincidence of time of the final breach with Rome to North and to South of the Border, though largely accidental, was of great consequence. The double event secured the unbroken permanence of the Reformation in both countries, and drew English and Scottish patriotism which had hither thriven on mutual hostility into an alliance of mutual defence....

'The Scottish Reformation was singularly bloodless, in spite of the violence of the language used on both sides. Very few Protestants had been burnt and no Catholic was executed on account of his religion. Continental Europe, and even England in Mary Tudor's reign, presented a far bloodier spectacle of religious fanaticism.'

The Reformation in England was comparatively slow, halting, and vacillating, ending with the Elizabethan Settlement in the choice of a middle path; a supreme example of what foreigners call the English muddle-headedness (if they use no harsher word), and of what Englishmen like to think of as the genius for compromise. In Scotland the Reformation, effected by the hammer strokes of John Knox bringing down the old Church and putting in its place the General Assembly, destroyed at once the possibility of such a subsequent artistic development as that which we are considering.

The English indecision and ultimate compromise enabled the bulk of the church composers to turn from Latin texts to English without any break in continuity, and in writing Services and Anthems for the cathedral establishments gradually to explore those problems of the language in which John Merbecke was a pioneer.

People have been puzzled to understand how it was that William Byrd, a devout Catholic, was able to retain his place in the Royal Chapel of Elizabeth and James I. It is not more puzzling than the fact that Merbecke, whose personal religion advanced to the extreme left of the Protestant party, was able to retain his post at Windsor through the reigns of both Mary and Elizabeth until his death. The Church of England was in fact preparing the way for that inclusiveness which to-day makes possible the existence of All Saints, Margaret Street, and All Souls, Langham Place, within a stone's throw of one another.

That Byrd, greatest of composers both for the Latin and the English offices, should be the progenitor of the English madrigal is evidence of that infiltration of cultural ideas from Italy which was possible under a sovereign who was herself an accomplished Latinist, a student of Italian literature, and the chief bulwark against the incursions of Papal aggression in the affairs of her country.

Though the madrigal form came from Italy and was directly imported in *Musica Transalpina*, a collection of Italian madrigals provided with English translations to which Byrd contributed two original specimens, it quickly acquired in the works of native composers the characteristics of their language. Byrd's first book, indeed, exhibits a good deal of the grave church style, partly due to the fact that it is the work of a man already arrived at middle age whose traditions were all those of the Church, and partly to the fact that lyrical poems amenable to the distinctive characteristics of the madrigal style were comparatively few in the language. In England it seems that the demand for madrigal music created the poetic form.[1] Nevertheless, the delicious gaiety of 'Though Amarylis dance in green', following the metrical translations of the Psalms,

---

[1] See *English Madrigal Verse*, collected and edited by E. H. Fellowes: Oxford University Press.

The Emergence of the Vernacular

distinctly belies the description of 'Songs of Sadness and Piety'.

In the later publications, however, both those of Byrd himself and those of his younger contemporaries, Morley (Byrd's pupil), Wilbye, and more particularly Thomas Weelkes, we find the rhythmic contours of the melodies increasingly 'framed to the life of the words', to quote Byrd's own expression.

To realize their freedom and their certainty we need to look at, or better still to sing, the several parts without the bar lines which modern editorship supplies for the convenience of choirmasters and singers, but which were not written in the original part-books. Take the following from Weelkes, for example. The principle will be found to be exactly the same as that of Merbecke, except that since Weelkes is writing for five contrapuntal voices a strict observance in the singing of the unit of measurement will be necessary, which Merbecke's unison did not call for.

The crotchet corresponds to Merbecke's 'Square' (unit of measurement), the minim to his 'Strene', and the quaver to his 'Pycke'. To bar it as four in the bar as the signature suggests is to produce false accents at the points marked *. The phrase swings perfectly if it is left alone as Weelkes wrote it.[1] In this way was the principle of 'just note and accent' interpreted, enabling the madrigal composers at the end of the sixteenth century and the beginning of the seventeenth to extract the expressive essence from lyrical words in every

[1] Fellowes here and throughout the *English Madrigal School* has adopted the plan of irregular barring in 4, 6, and 3 as occasion serves.

mood and reproduce every subtlety of rhythmic form which the English language possesses.

While the typical madrigal poetry of the era was devised round the fantastic imagery of the idyllic love-scene with the pastoral figures of Phyllis and Corydon as protagonists, there are many pieces which touch on deeper emotions and express a more personal standpoint. Nowhere is that more consistently discernible than in the work of Orlando Gibbons, the short-lived composer who belonged to a generation later than that of most of the great madrigalists, and in whose single volume there is a fastidiousness in the choice of poems which makes him representative of what may be called a romantic tendency following the classical era. While Byrd, Morley, and Weelkes can find their musical inspiration anywhere, Gibbons searches out words which reflect his own temperament. He lived and worked when the decay of the Elizabethan art and literature was imminent. He deplored 'the learned poets', he found a symbolism in the 'dainty fine bird' encaged. His masterpiece is Raleigh's Stoic poem, 'What is our life?' with its disillusioned ending 'Only we die in earnest that's no jest'. His melancholy, reflective spirit responds quickly to satire. If his 'Silver Swan' be placed beside that of Arcadelt the dropping fifths of its last line contrast with Arcadelt's rising fourths as strongly as does the conclusion of the poem itself.

> Farewell all joys, O death come close mine eyes.
> More geese than swans now live, more fools than wise.

CHAPTER III
'STILE RAPPRESENTATIVO'

AMONG the madrigals of whatever nation there are some of which one feels that the polyphonic texture, the many voices contributing to a single idea, is not quite the right thing. The *chanson* of di Lasso and Gibbons's 'The Silver Swan' are both cases in point, though for different reasons. We feel instinctively that the petulance of the young wife's complaint of her husband could be made more vivid with less paraphernalia, that a soliloquy of any sort should be sung by a single voice. It is a fragment of drama requiring direct representation in the person of the speaker or singer. The case of Gibbons is a little more elusive. The composer is speaking his own mind, not identifying himself with another's. The subjective standpoint has entered into his art. The emotion of the work of art has become a personal communication from the artist to the hearer.

In using the words 'romantic' and 'classical' to distinguish Gibbons from his predecessors I was applying to his case terms which are generally associated with the change which occurred between the standpoint towards the arts of the eighteenth century and that of the nineteenth. To take a familiar example in music, we find Mozart well content to bestow his genius on such irresponsible comedies of intrigue as *Figaro* and *Don Giovanni*, while Beethoven cast about for opera subjects which should chime with his own ethical ideals and accepted such an inferior one as *Fidelio* because it gave him opportunity to pour out his art on ideas of freedom and faithfulness, while Wagner, going a step further, had to write his own words in order that every detail might express his personal conviction. Thus subjectivity grew in what is known as the romantic era succeeding the classical.

Two hundred years earlier the same tendencies made

their appearance and were not confined to the minor case of Gibbons; indeed, they were only vaguely felt in the England of Gibbons's day. While the polyphonic madrigal was still in its heyday the active minds of the Italian Renaissance were seeking for a wholly different and more personal means of musical expression and were speculating in what they called the *stile rappresentativo*. The bulk of madrigal poetry clung to impersonal types, gave vent to human emotions generalized as it were by association with classical characters and accepted images, things which could be suitably expressed by the co-operation of several voices singing dispersedly and contrapuntally. But the artist wants to get further than that; if his theme is love, he wants to deal, not only in the collective emotions, joys, and sorrows of lovers, but in the individual ones of particular lovers in their several situations, real or imagined—in the last resort of his own. And the more his work is individualized the more generally attractive it is likely to become to the mass of his audience. That is why the novel exercises a perennial fascination, so that in the modern industry of literature it is the novelists who compete in the production of 'best sellers'. In music, as in the drama or acted novel, there is also the personality of the performer to be taken into account.[1] It can reinforce or neutralize that of the composer, and act so powerfully on the listener as often to deprive him of all critical estimate of the work performed.[2] Hence it comes that no amount of wise advice will persuade the average audience that the *ensemble* piece of music is more worthy of its applause than the ballad sung by a singer of commanding presence.

It was the urgent desire to express themselves as individuals calling in the aid of the singer's individuality which set the Italians to work in the direction of the *stile rappresentativo*. By it they meant the telling of a story

[1] On this question see *Music and Psychology*, by Frank Howes.
[2] Cf. *The Scope of Music*, p. 58.

Stile Rappresentativo

in music, not necessarily associated with the stage, with all the vividness to be gained from the characters being represented each by a single voice with the support of a more or less independent instrumental accompaniment. Solo song there had always been, but this was to be something larger and at the same time more intimate than the ballad in which the same tune served indifferently the purposes of different verses. This representative music had to follow the words line by line and clause by clause. The voice was to be free to concentrate on declamation; the instrumental accompaniment, whether that of a single instrument such as lute or bass viol, or of instruments in consort such as a group of viols, had to supply the expressive suggestions of harmony, which under the influence of vocal polyphony had grown by this time from a luxury into a necessity of the normal ear.

The style passed through its experimental stages more or less under cover of the highly developed polyphonic music of the sixteenth century, so much so that historians have made the mistake of supposing that the little group of poets and composers, who about the year 1600 met in Florence and set themselves to produce works according to theories which they formulated on the subject, were creating a complete revolution in musical principles. Actually, the *Nuove Musiche* of Caccini recalled principles which we have already seen to be at the root of all vocal music, and the musical plays, mostly on the subject of Orpheus and Euridice, which the Florentines produced, summed up sporadic attempts in a similar direction which had been made at intervals throughout the Renaissance period, attempts to join music with poetry outside the purely lyrical forms.[1]

The *stile rappresentativo* naturally found its richest opportunity in connexion with stage plays, although such things as the musical recitation of sonnets, elegies, and odes contributed to it. Two forms of especial importance to us grew out of it, the opera and the oratorio, and the

---
[1] See *Forerunners of Italian Opera*, by J. W. Henderson.

artistic impulses which produced these forms are worth consideration at a time when both are being called in question.

There is to-day no more popular form of dispute than that between the attackers and defenders of opera and oratorio. People who are rather tired of listening to repeated performances of Handel's *Messiah* and Mendelssohn's *Elijah* call the oratorio an outworn and jejune form of art; others point to the practice of making people sing on the stage what they would say in ordinary life as irrational, and assert with the air of having produced a clinching argument that for their part if they want a play they prefer to go to the ordinary theatre and that if they want music they go to a concert. There are those who think the opera rather wicked because of its customary association with the theme of sexual love, and who find the oratorio rather edifying because of its customary association with Biblical narrative. On the other hand, there are those who find the opera entertaining and the oratorio dull, possibly for the same reasons. If we realize that both spring from the same impulse in the artist, to say something which he could not say in any other way, and admit that there may be good and bad operas and good and bad oratorios, and also that we as individuals have a right to our own preferences, even among the good specimens of either class, we shall also perceive the futility of condemning either as a form of art.[1]

Take the case of the man who first produced an enduring work in opera. We may see by reference to Claudio Monteverdi's *Orfeo* what it was which made him turn from the composition of madrigals to the *stile rappresentativo*. The opera was produced at the court of Mantua in 1607, when its composer was already some forty years of age. Evidently exceptional resources were at his disposal for the occasion, for the cast of singers is a large one, the demands made on their technical ability, especially on the representative of

[1] Cf. *The Scope of Music*, p. 49, on 'The nature of beauty'.

Stile Rappresentativo

Orpheus, are enormous, a considerable choir is required in conjunction with the solo singers, and almost every known instrument is included in the heterogeneous orchestra. The opera opens with a vigorous fanfare of brass; a quintet of viols plays interludes; harpsichords, lutes, and occasionally organs participate in the accompaniment of the solo voices, and there are *obbligato* parts for violins, a flute, and other instruments. A suggestion of the general style may be best conveyed by a description of one scene, the first of many of poignant emotion—that in which Orpheus receives the news of Euridice's death. Monteverdi's object is to heighten the effect of the sudden blow by contrast with the serenity of that which precedes it. With that in view Orpheus, seated among the shepherds on the hill-side or in the open glade, is given a lyrical song in praise of his 'bella Euridice', four verses set to a flowing care-free melody repeated to each one of them, with an interlude for strings between each. A shepherd replies to him in a scarcely less lyrical vein, rejoicing in the beauty of nature and exhorting him,

> Haste thee then with plectrum of gold
> To soothe the zephyrs of this blessed morning.[1]

With a change of time from the perfect (triple) to the imperfect (common), the voice of the messenger laments the cruel fate (*fat'empio e crudele*) which has befallen. The sombre tones of the organ are added to the accompaniment of harpsichord and lute.

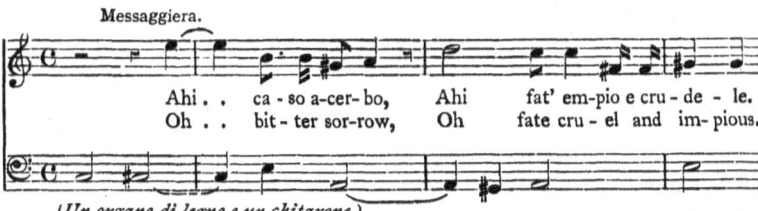

[1] The phrases of English translation here quoted are taken from that of Mr. R. L. Stuart written for the revival of *Orfeo* at Oxford in December 1925. The musical score used is that edited by Malipiero, but the quotations do not include Malipiero's filling up of the harmony.

The attention of all is arrested, their mirth invaded. In the conversation which follows between the messenger, Orpheus, and the shepherd, carried on in recitative (that is to say, music in which the declamation of the words alone decides the time of the notes), the delay in the delivery of the news of death by question and interjection, is exceedingly skilful. This is the art of drama. In real life the anxious man says, 'What has happened?' and gets his answer, except in that class of society which believes in breaking things gently. In the drama, and especially in music-drama, the situation takes time to develop if the emotional significance is to be fully grasped. It is not the fact of Euridice's death but its effect on Orpheus which has to be brought home to the audience, and it is thus that the work of art differs from real life, so that all appeals to realism are irrelevant as criticism of the work of art. Even in the moment of enlightenment Orpheus's interjection delays the words of death.

Stile Rappresentativo

Monteverdi attempts a graphic detail of expression by changing the mode, putting Orpheus's words into a flat key in contrast to the messenger's in a sharp one. The juxtaposition of the chords of E major and E flat is not skilfully managed; the device is rather beyond the composer's harmonic technique, but his intention is clear. He wants Orpheus's interjection to appear like a dramatic 'aside' and the voice of the messenger to pick up exactly where it left off, ignoring the interruption.

The crucial fact once stated, the messenger enters on a narration of how Euridice met her death, at the end of which it is the shepherd who first takes up the lament, using both the words 'Ahi caso acerbo' and the musical phrase (see p. 41) of the messenger. Orpheus's own lament is pitched lower, and with its organ accompaniment suggests a deeper grief than that of the sympathetic onlookers. Finally, the whole chorus takes up the tale and the scene is rounded off with one of those outbursts of five-part choral writing which reminds us that Monteverdi's *stile rappresentativo* has grown out of his mastery of the madrigal style. Here it should be noticed that what may be called the grief motive forms the bass of the chorus.

Even this cursory analysis will show that Monteverdi disposes the several musical elements, from the lyrical song to the choral lament with the dramatic dialogue between them, to give effect at once to a dramatic and a musical design. His knowledge of the arts of the musical dramatist seems almost uncanny, for his work illustrates every canon of the art for which both Gluck and Wagner fought centuries later. The music bodies forth the 'states of the souls' of the protagonists; it reinforces the drama without delaying its movement; at the same time it has a life of its own, even to the embryonic use of that Wagnerian device of the representative theme.

It is little wonder that the vogue of this new music became tremendous and that in the later years of Monteverdi's life (1637) the first public opera-house was opened and became a popular institution in Venice, in which city Monteverdi had settled and where he wrote his later works. In becoming an institution the opera naturally attracted to itself all sorts and conditions of musical artists, composers, singers, and instrumentalists, and what came into existence as an intuitive stroke of genius tended to be carried on as an industry. The history of Italian opera after Monteverdi is one of steadily encroaching conventions, some of them practically useful, others palpably absurd, but all accepted as a means of organizing the companies of performers and satisfying the demands of audiences, often at the expense of the creative artist's initial impulse. The orchestra was soon reduced to more manageable proportions, principal singers were distinguished from secondary ones, the reign of the *prima donna* and *primo uomo* began and induced that insistence on the purely lyrical parts of the music which made Italian opera a century later little more than a series of arias, strung together on a slight thread of conversational narrative told in purely conventional recitative.

We need not follow its history into these phases, but merely note parenthetically that the incentive given to the style by Monteverdi did not stop in Italy, but was carried to Paris by his pupil Cavalli, who sowed a seed there which propagated and grew into the French opera cultivated by Lully at the Court of Louis XIV. Further, I would remind you that the singer-ridden opera of Italy in the latter part of the century produced two things for which the whole art of music is indebted to

Stile Rappresentativo

it—perfection in the art of singing and the aria-form itself. From these two things the instrumental sonata took its rise; as I suggested in the first chapter, the violin arrived to emulate the voice, and the sonata for it was an expansion of those principles of contrast of key to which the aria-form first gave currency.[1]

The companion form of oratorio only differs from opera in one fundamental feature. It is the application of the *stile rappresentativo* to a story which is not enacted before the eyes of an audience, and this brings in the need for some means of telling those parts of a story which are not made clear in the conversation of the several characters. This is made evident in the familiar case of the Passion Music of J. S. Bach. If Bach had been setting to music a Passion Play he would have had no need of a narrator to read aloud musically the story as told by the Evangelist. The seventeenth-century oratorios of Carissimi exhibit this feature in common with Bach, and it is evident that in both of them the art of musical recitation is applied to a less directly emotional end than it is in the dramatic recitative of Monteverdi.

A glance at the progress of German Passion Music, from the time when it meant the intoning of the Gospel story with plainsong inflexions as part of the Holy Week ritual of the Catholic Church to Bach's oratorio-like treatment of it, will make this clear. As early as the twelfth century the custom of distributing the words of the Saviour and other persons of the story between the several ministrants at the Altar introduced the dramatic principle into the ritual. In the fifteenth century a composer, Johann Obrecht, wrote four-part choruses to be sung by the choir representing the interjections of the crowd. Many later composers of all countries, including our own William Byrd, wrote similar choruses in the manner of the Latin motet to be sung in conjunction with the traditional recitation, each embodying his own con-

[1] See *Alessandro Scarlatti*, by E. J. Dent.

ception of the words of the crowd in the scenes of the trials and the Crucifixion of our Saviour. Thus far and no further the composers could express themselves within the limits of the liturgy of the Catholic Church.

Lutheran Germany, with the vernacular text of the Gospels and the chorale as a means of congregational devotion devised by Luther himself, as I mentioned in the last chapter, could go much further. Heinrich Schütz (1585–1672), taking a hint from Italy, replaced traditional plainsong forms with a more articulate recitative; he also wrote opening and closing choruses independent of the actual narrative. Other composers made further innovations such as contemplative arias or solo songs commenting, like the chorales, on the various episodes of the sacred story, and ultimately the Biblical text itself was abandoned in favour of what may be described as metrical *libretti*, of which one by a certain man named Brockes was set by several composers, including Handel.

Thus the tradition of Passion Music which J. S. Bach received and which he clarified in his two masterpieces and transferred to other subjects than Passion Music, notably the Christmas Oratorio, was twofold; it was half-dramatic narrative and half-devotional contemplation. It is of the essence of opera that emotion should be expressed in the course of the action and through the characters involved in the action. In oratorio the narrative and the emotion it arouses may be taken alternately. Bach in his narrative generally aims at no more than a general expressiveness comparable to the rise and fall of the voice in intelligent reading. It is only in exceptional moments such as 'And Peter went out and wept bitterly' or 'Eloi, Eloi lama sabachthani' that he rouses himself to an intense and poignant musical expression in his recitative. Even the supreme examples of Bach suggest that there is a weakness inherent in the oratorio form which in lesser hands has in fact brought disaster. It is the danger that the composer and the

Stile Rappresentativo

audience alike may take the story for granted, that the audience may accept it for reasons quite outside the province of art, allowing their feelings of piety or sense of edification to take the place of any direct appeal made by the artistic presentation of it, and the composer, relying on this attitude in his hearers, may be content with a perfunctory treatment of the words. That has been the pitfall into which many able English composers and their public have fallen, and it accounts for the innumerable still-born works following the mighty output of Handel, which almost seem to justify the uncritical assertion that oratorio is a dead thing.

Returning to the question of setting words in musical recitative, it may be pointed out that there is a legitimate place both in oratorio and opera for the dispassionate statement. Opera composers, especially those of romantic tendencies, have erred as much in the impassioned delivery of the obvious as oratorio composers have in the unimpassioned treatment of the sublime. It was one of the virtues of the classical school of Italian opera from Alessandro Scarlatti to Mozart that its members knew so well how to carry on the necessary converse of its characters with a light musical touch which avoided over-emphasis. In oratorio Handel's 'There were Shepherds' (*Messiah*) is a supreme instance of an aptly placed dispassionate statement. Any more elaborate outline than the simple intonation mostly on adjacent notes would have anticipated the event of the angelic vision in the words 'And the glory of the Lord shone round about them'.

There are innumerable instances of a similar restraint preparing the way for the emotional moment in Bach's recitative, but it must be admitted, I think, that the need for carrying on the long narrative passages of the Passion story in this manner developed certain habits in him which blunted his sense of fitness. Bach's recitative has been universally admired and Handel's generally has been sharply criticized. We shall examine Handel's treatment of the English language in oratorio more particularly at a later stage. Here I shall venture on a heresy with regard to Bach and suggest that his narrative recitative has been overpraised. It is true that he discovered how to adapt the recitative of the Italians to the ruder accent of the German tongue, but in reading his Lutheran Bible aloud in music he acquired a sing-song tone of voice. He was apt to read it more like the educated parson than like the sensitive artist. We find him reading very different things in practically the same musical phraseology. The defect becomes an absurdity when he turns from his Bible to some secular, indeed frivolous, piece of literature and proceeds to deliver it in the Biblical tone of voice.

Stile Rappresentativo 49

These two passages are taken from the *Christmas Oratorio* and the comic cantata *Der Streit zwischen Phoebus und Pan*. Play and sing them without their words and it would be impossible to tell which is preparing to recount the mystery of the Incarnation and which is the satire on the presumptuous claims of the grotesque goat-god. They display the same harmonious progressions and the voice runs to and fro over arpeggios of the chosen chords with only incidental reference to the verbal accentuation. I purposely choose a passage from the oratorio in which the words are a plain statement of fact, having in themselves little or no emotional significance, and place it beside one which is meant to introduce us to the impertinent character of Pan boasting of his musical prowess to Phoebus. The comparison shows how little of a dramatist Bach was, since he could be content to give so little distinction to Pan's utterances. It also shows him giving much more inflexion than is needed by the facts of Joseph's itinerary. Handel shows a finer sense of values in his 'There were Shepherds', which may also be compared with Bach's setting of the same words in the *Christmas Oratorio*, a setting which again sprawls over wide arpeggios in the manner of the examples given above.

Bach indeed, secure in the acceptance of the narrative by a pietistic audience, did little in this part of his work beyond finding a serviceable formula which would carry him safely over the ground without the exercise of much thought over each individual passage. Where the words or the situation really moved him he invented far more subtle methods by means of a recitative accompanied by orchestral instruments which merges into the aria-style without the aria-form. The supreme instance of this is his setting of the words of the Saviour in the institution of the Last Supper in the *Matthaeus Passion*, the beauty and fitness of which is instantly apparent to every listener.

In Bach's day German opera hardly existed, and indeed the language had to wait more than another hundred years before a style of musical declamation wholly supple and malleable to its needs was achieved in the music drama of Wagner. Bach in his accompanied recitatives and arioso numbers of the *Matthaeus Passion* forestalled that style to a remarkable extent. To place the passage above alluded to beside the similar consecration scene in *Parsifal* is to realize that Wagner consciously or unconsciously worked with tools which Bach had fashioned for him.

CHAPTER IV
TOWARDS ENGLISH OPERA

If music and sweet poetry agree
As they needs must, the sister and the brother,
Then must the love be great twixt thee and me
Because thou lov'st the one and I the other.

Dowland to thee is dear, whose heavenly touch
Upon the lute doth ravish human sense;
Spenser to me, whose deep conceit is such,
As passing all conceit needs no defence.

Thou lov'st to hear the sweet melodious sound
That Phoebus' lute, the Queen of Music, makes;
And I in deep delight am chiefly drowned
Whenas himself to singing he betakes.

One god is god of both as poets feign;
One Knight loves both, and both in thee remain.[1]

WHO was this Dowland whom the sonneteer ranks beside Edmund Spenser, poet of *The Faerie Queene*, and what was this lute which is described as the 'Queen of Music'? The question, though no doubt many could get full marks in answering both parts of it, may not be entirely superfluous, for great composers in this country are generally much less famous than great poets, and innumerable congregations join in Psalm cl with enthusiasm, exhorting each other to 'Praise Him upon the lute and harp', without ever inquiring about the nature of the former instrument.[2]

Considering that the lute was to the musicians of the Renaissance very much what the pianoforte is to musicians to-day, an elementary knowledge of what it looked like and of the way in which it made music is necessary if we are to get into touch with their outlook on their art. Imagine for a moment the case of people, living perhaps four hundred years hence, who had

[1] Sonnet by Richard Barnfield, early seventeenth century, often ascribed to Shakespeare.
[2] While I was preparing these lectures for the press a lady standing in her drawing-room with her back to a reproduction of one of Melozzo da Forli's angels with a lute, which had stood on her mantelpiece for years, asked me in complete innocence, 'What *is* a lute?'

entirely forgotten what a pianoforte is. What chance would they have of appreciating the music of the nineteenth century? Vocal music, which is perennial, would be open to them; the orchestra, from the symphonies of Beethoven to the symphonic poems of Richard Strauss, would be at least translatable into their modern terms. But the sonatas of Beethoven, the songs of Schubert, the whole of Chopin, large tracts of Schumann, Brahms, Debussy, would have so fallen into desuetude that it would be almost impossible to get at the minds of these masters. That is what has happened to Dowland and to innumerable other artists of his time and before it, Italian, Spanish, French, and English, whose names are practically forgotten. Dowland was a virtuoso of his instrument and wrote much solo music for it. Being also a singer, he wrote his own songs and sang them to his own lute accompaniment.

Our sonnet suggests that the person addressed was devoted to instrumental music, while the writer was more moved by song because of its union of 'music and sweet poetry'.

The lute was in fact a stringed instrument built in many different sizes and strung with a varying number of strings according to its size. It is pictured in so many Italian paintings that its appearance must be familiar to many people who have never troubled to connect with the name the beautiful pear-shaped instrument thrumbed by infant angels seated at the feet of the Holy Families of Bellini, Raphael, and others.

These small lutes had six strings tuned normally in fourths with a third between the third and fourth strings. The playing of the open strings gives that ungainly succession of notes with which Wagner makes fun in *Die Meistersinger* when Beckmesser, lute in hand, comes to serenade Eva.

Wagner. "Die Meistersinger," Act II.

Towards English Opera

Dowland's song accompaniments show that he used a seven-stringed lute, but the six-stringed one will serve to explain the technique and the way of writing the music. The music for the lute was written according to a 'tablature', that is to say a representation (or tabulation) of what the player must *do*. Ordinary notation is a representation of what the musician (primarily the singer) must *think*.[1]

This wants a little explanation. The finger-board of the lute was fretted in semitones. Place the finger against the first fret and the note which was G becomes G sharp, against the second fret and the note becomes A, and so on. Dowland's tablature used letters to represent the frets; 'a' was the open note, 'b' the first fret, 'c' the second; thus the letters up to 'h' represented the ascending chromatic scale on one string through the course of a perfect fifth, as follows:

Open notes.

a	
b	½ tone higher.
c	1 tone.
d	1½ tones (minor 3rd).
e	2 tones (major 3rd).
f	2½ tones (perfect 4th).
g	3 tones (augmented 4th).
h	3½ tones (perfect 5th).

These actions of the left-hand fingers on the strings were expressed graphically by means of what looks like a six-lined stave but is not really a stave at all. The spaces between the lines represent the strings, and in

---

[1] Players of Jazz music on the modern ukelele will readily grasp this because they in fact play from a tablature which shows them where to place their fingers on the strings in order to produce the required chords. They are saved from thinking anything; they have merely to follow out the directions and the chords come.

those spaces are placed the letters which represent the fingering according to the frets.

The following specimen from the song 'Dear, if you change' may be read in conjunction with the table given above:

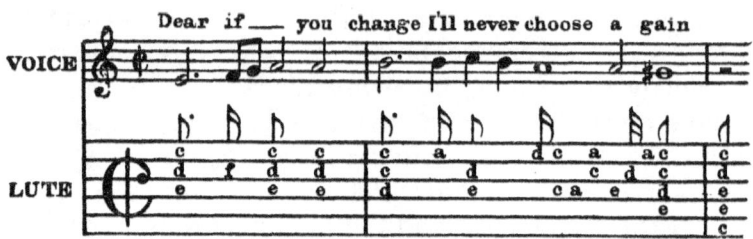

The signs above the lines look to musicians like headless quavers and semiquavers, to others they look more like railway signals set at 'safety'. The latter is the better description of them. They show how fast the notes may move; the notes are to go at the pace the signal indicates until the next one is reached. If, therefore, we take it that

        ⌐ = semibreve pace
        ▶ = minim pace
        ▶ = crotchet pace
        ▶ = quaver pace,

we get the following transliteration into ordinary notation of the passage quoted:

The point in the long second bar where the music begins to move at crotchet pace looks pretty formless, as though the notes were dropped out at haphazard without any horizontal connexion. One must remember, however, that this represents the plucking of the notes, and that the strings unchecked would continue to vibrate until another note on the same string was plucked. Hence the low F would sound on through the B and D but would cease with the A which is on the same string.

Towards English Opera 55

The passage, then, might be accurately rendered by

which looks a little more shapely. What it implies, translating into terms of voice-parts, is

three voices entering in turn on a point of imitation. It was left to the 'touch' of the lutenist to bring out such a detail of the form, just as a pianist by careful part-playing must bring out the entries in a fugue, the only difference being that the pianist has the parts written for him according to their sense, the lutenist had the notes written only for his 'information ănd necessary action', as a government official would say.

This simple illustration will show what a wealth of difference there was between the bad lutenist who simply acted according to instructions and the 'heavenly touch' of a Dowland. My purpose in going into the detail of the lute's technique is to suggest to you that the lute, like the pianoforte, was susceptible to personal interpretation in a way which its successors, the virginal and harpsichord, were not. Incidentally it offers an instance of how musical sense is discovered by referring the instrumental passage to vocal standards (see Chapter I). The lute, like the later keyboard instruments, gave to a single performer the means of translating into instrumental terms the implications (though not necessarily all the facts) of vocal harmony. It was quiet in tone and therefore fit to accompany the voice. It was susceptible to subtle variations of loud and soft, capable of accent and of *nuance*, and therefore interesting to the musical ear when heard by itself.[1] Further, the chromatic nature of its technique and tablature

---

[1] The guitar playing of Señor Segovia is the nearest modern equivalent to the 'heavenly touch' on the lute.

should be noticed. Staff notation is essentially diatonic. Chromatic notes have to be put in by means of accidentals. Very often they were not put in; what was called 'musica ficta' was left to the judgement of the individual singer. Editors of sixteenth-century vocal music often have great difficulty in deciding whether a note is intended to be natural or sharp. The lutenist's fingering made him think in semitones, and lute-playing was probably directly responsible[1] for the increased chromaticism of vocal music at the end of the century. The lute tablature being written in semitones, there is no doubt in our example as to the use of G sharp and G natural.

The name of John Dowland stands for us as representative of the lute and its music, because, by his personal genius enriched by experience in the course of wide continental travels, he made the solo song with lute accompaniment a power in English music just at the time when the concerted madrigal was at its height. His career abroad has been traced[2] from an early visit to Paris in 1580, when he was about eighteen, through 'the chiefest parts of France', and later in Germany, Italy, Poland, and Denmark. He returned to England at intervals and spent some time here, taking a musical degree at Oxford (1588) and applying unsuccessfully for an appointment at court. Religious difficulties may have stood in his way, and it is certain that the favours lavished on him by foreign potentates, the friendship of leading continental musicians, and what we now call the 'artistic atmosphere' of other lands, served to make foreign residence more congenial than England was to Dowland. England is always in trouble for not taking

---

[1] The excessive chromaticism of such a composer as Gesualdo di Venosa in madrigal writing suggests a comparison with those twentieth-century composers who base their work on the twelve semitones to an octave of the equal temperament pianoforte.

[2] See Barclay Squire's article in *Grove's Dictionary of Music and Musicians*.

Towards English Opera

her musical sons[1] and daughters quite at their own valuation.

The all-important fact is, however, that he wrote his songs to English texts (possibly he was poet as well as musician) and began to publish them here in books of twenty-one numbers in 1597. This was the year when Morley's *Plaine and Easie Introduction to Practicall Musick* came out, and the time when all England was discovering its musical capability through the printing press. Part-books of the madrigals were being sold to every country-house party much as gramophone records are sold to-day, though with the important difference in result that the members of the sixteenth-century country-house parties sang the madrigals, whereas those of the twentieth century have only to fix a needle and turn a handle. In view of the prevalence of part-singing, Dowland's 'First book of Ayres' and the subsequent ones were published in two versions, the solos with lute accompaniments, as presumably he sang them himself, and an arrangement for four voices which could be sung without the lute.[2]

It was the accompanied solo which brought a new element into English music, but it is to be noticed that Dowland's songs and his performance of them were a thing quite distinct from that impulse towards the *stile rappresentativo*, which at this very moment was precipitating revolution in Italian song. Dowland's songs are as lyrical as the madrigal itself. Both words and music are singularly free from that tendency towards subjectivity verging on drama discussed at the beginning of the previous chapter. Most of them are love songs, but they are any lover to his lady. The woes of love

[1] If Dowland was an Irishman, as Dr. Grattan Flood asserts, that helps to explain his dissatisfaction with England; it also acquits England of responsibility towards him. He certainly showed no more desire to live in Ireland than do great Irish artists to-day.

[2] The solo versions with lute of all Dowland's four song-books are published in several volumes of *The English School of Lutenist Song-writers*, edited by E. H. Fellowes (Stainer and Bell).

predominate because it was the flattering fashion of the time (flattering to the lady, that is) to sing

> How shall I then gaze on my mistress' eye. ?
> My thoughts must have some vent, else heart will break.

The manlier tone of the one chosen here for illustration is comparatively rare:

> Dear, if you change, I'll never choose again;
> Sweet, if you shrink, I'll never think of love;
> Fair, if you fail, I'll judge all beauty vain;
> Wise, if too weak, more wits I'll never prove.
>> Dear, Sweet, Fair, Wise, change, shrink, nor be not weak,
>> And on my faith, my faith shall never break!

The eighty odd songs of Dowland are a mine of pure melody; the supple outlines bend to the suggestions and accents of the words. Note how in the refrain the epithets with which each line began are declaimed on a single note, and also the fact that a similar series of the elements in the second verse makes the lyric particularly suitable for the strophic form.

> Earth, Heaven, Fire, Air, the world transformed shall view,
> Ere I prove false to faith, or strange to you.

This quotation leads me to recall to you the principle of rhythmic accentuation without bars discussed above

---

[1] The lute part is transcribed here strictly in accordance with the terms of the tablature. Fellowes (*English School of Lutenist Song-writers*, vol. i) gives a realization of the implied polyphony of the lute part.

Towards English Opera

(p. 35) in connexion with the madrigal by Weelkes. Clearly Dowland's method, though these bar-lines are his own, is essentially at one with that of the madrigalists. The bar-lines inserted irregularly are put in to help the eye and keep voice and instrument together. The beginning of the bar implies no accent; if it did, that six-minim bar would be the most ridiculous piece of 'ragtime'. Without such an accent it is a perfect piece of verbal accentuation.

This brings us to that essential change of attitude towards rhythm which cuts the history of music in two at the beginning of the seventeenth century, and affects the setting of the English language so closely that it is absolutely necessary to grasp its implications, if we are to carry our inquiry a stage farther and bridge the gulf between Dowland and Purcell. We can do this best by considering again, as we did in the case of Merbecke, what were the practical conditions which musicians had to meet.

Dowland's practical conditions were simple and ideal. With his lute in his hand and his song in his head he could give exactly that lilt to vocal and instrumental parts in one which made 'music and sweet poetry agree'. Every musician of the older generation to-day remembers the unique charm which Sir George Henschel used to give to songs of Schubert and of Brahms by his singing of them to his own pianoforte accompaniment, and it is always the aim of the recitalist and his accompanist to reach a unanimity of conception which can rival the art of the single performer.

Dowland set a fashion in songs to the lute which was copied by other composers. Their songs were doubtless sung by many singers who were not lutenists and possibly accompanied by lutenists who were not singers. Moreover, songs of their type, and indeed many of the actual specimens which are published in the books of the poet-musician Thomas Campian, found their way into the masques which were the fashionable form of entertainment for amateur actors, dancers, and musicians in the Jacobean and first Caroline era. It is easy to imagine the confusion which would result when music like Dowland's was attempted in the course of so elaborate an entertainment as the masque. The singer, in costume and singing perhaps with a certain amount of action, would be on the floor of the great hall, while one or more musicians, with lute, bass viol, or other instruments at a distance from him, would probably be placed in a gallery or some out-of-the-way corner. A common accent at regular intervals through the song would become a necessity, and the principle which kept the steps of the dancers in time with their music would naturally be applied to singer and accompaniment. In fact it became necessary to beat time, not to the eye as the modern conductor does with a stick, but to the ear with an accent on the first of the bar. Composers who ignored the necessity and continued to write such phrases as Dowland's 'And on my faith' did so at their peril. No doubt amateur performers woefully misaccented such delicate rhythmic shapes in their frantic efforts, aided by head-wagging and foot-stamping, to keep together. The widespread popularity of these various forms of concerted music, whether in madrigal or masque, suggests that a fairly low standard of *ensemble* must have been considered good enough, for there is no reason to suppose that averagely educated English men and women were more sensitive to such niceties then than now, and it is absurd to suppose that they did by the light of nature what our modern *ensemble* parties of the competitive festivals can do only by a process of intensive drilling under an expert conductor.

The delicate arts of the madrigal-writer and of the lutenist song-writer must have been frequently degraded in performance by the half-educated amateurs for whom Morley wrote his *Plaine and Easie Introduc-*

tion; evidently their rhythmic principles broke down altogether in practice when transferred to the masque with its many distractions of stagecraft and pageantry to prevent the performers from concentration on their musical task.

In short, though words and music were well combined in the writing, they were all awry in the singing, and it was the performance not the composition which justified John Milton's diatribe against the 'Midas ears, committing short for long'. Milton's own father, be it remembered, was no mean composer in the madrigal style, and the poet was perfectly aware of what the principles of that style were; it was the practice he objected to.

Henry Lawes was a practical man, not a lyrical genius like Dowland. As a capable singer, Gentleman of the Chapel Royal, with a gift for organization, he was engaged to run the musical side of the court masques at the time when their need of direction was most evident. Both John Dowland and Orlando Gibbons had died, the latter prematurely, at the beginning of Charles I's reign. Thomas Campian, whose lute songs were of a simpler and more manageable kind than Dowland's, was also dead. There was a distinct dearth of original musicianship. Tentative attempts had been made to introduce something like the new Italian recitative into the masque music. They had not been successful. The English amateurs wanted a tune. The poets wanted their lines to be heard. Lawes saw how to do it and supplied the felt want. He accepted the regular accent of the bar as a musical necessity, he felt the metrical accents of the lines and proceeded to nail the two firmly together in his masquing airs. The plan worked; singers and players were easily able to keep touch with one another; the complaints of the poets were turned to praise of his skill.[1]

---

[1] See, besides the sonnet of Milton, Herrick's poem on 'Mr. H. Lawes, his Airs'.

'Comus', a masque produced at Ludlow Castle for the Earl of Bridgwater in 1634 is the most famous of the many entertainments which Lawes organized, because in it his music was 'married to immortal verse'. Milton was induced to write it partly by his wish to gratify Lawes and prove his friendship for this friend of poets, partly by a hope of giving a more edifying character to the society craze for masques. His virtue would replace their wantonness with an ennobling theme of chastity. If his moral purpose hardly attained its immediate end, his artistic one more than justified the excursion of the Puritan into the ways of the theatre by producing a poem of imperishable beauty. Milton, indeed, showed himself to be as little of a dramatist in his poetry as was J. S. Bach in his music. His attitude towards his theme is almost entirely contemplative. He asked very little co-operation from the musician. 'Soft music' at the setting out of Comus's feast is named, and the performance of some country-dancers is allowed for in the *finale*. In the course of the work there are five songs, the Lady's 'Sweet Echo', the Spirit's invocation of 'Sabrina fair', Sabrina's reply, 'By the rushy-fringed bank', the Spirit's dismissal of the dancers, 'Back, Shepherds', and his presentation of his charges to their parents, 'Noble Lord, and Lady bright'. None of them are ideal for musical setting according to lyrical standards; they have little contrast of mood and each is packed with a verbal imagery which makes it complete without any musical addition. The view ascribed to Stravinsky (quoted in Chapter I), that a fine poem gains nothing by being set to music, becomes intelligible here. There is a certain sort of fine poem which leaves little for the musician to add, and Milton's songs in 'Comus' are of that sort. Lawes set them dutifully. He devised a melodic declamation for the lines in which every metrical accent found its counterpart in his bar accent, a primary one on the first beat and

Towards English Opera 63

a secondary one on the third. 'Sabrina fair' shows his method:

    — ᴗ | — | —   ᴗ | — ᴗ | — ᴗ |
Sabrina fair, Listen where thou art sitting

| —   ᴗ | — ᴗ | —   ᴗ | — ᴗ | —
Under the grassie, cool, translucent wave,

ᴗ | — ᴗ | —   ᴗ | — ᴗ | — ᴗ
In twisted braids of lilies knitting

ᴗ | —   ᴗ | — ᴗ | —   ᴗ | —
The loose train of thy amber dropping hair,

— ᴗ | — ᴗ | — ᴗ | —
Listen, for dear honour's sake,

—   ᴗ | — ᴗ | — ᴗ | —
Goddess of the silver lake.

Analysis will show how consistently Lawes's bars accord with the scansion. His melody will sometimes break through the mechanical uniformity by an anticipation (the voice entering on the fourth beat and held over, as with 'cool') or by the reverse process of delaying the vocal entry till the accent is passed, as with 'In twisted braids'; but in general the metre is so closely adhered to that even the prepositions 'for' and 'of', if they happen to fall on the 'long' of the foot are placed on an accent of the bar.

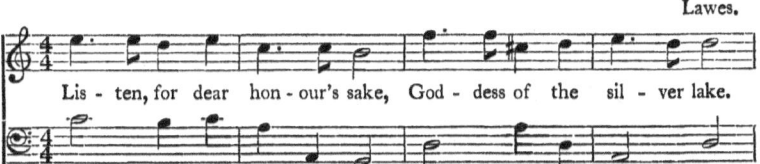

This did not offend Milton because it made his couplet scan; it does offend us who realize that the musical setting of words demands the reconciliation of three concomitants (poetic metre, speech rhythm, and musical time, see Chapter I) while he was content with two. Lawes here is as bad as Elgar in 'The Shepherd' (see p. 16).

This sample shows conclusively what Lawes achieved and what he left to be done by a later generation of English composers. The dramatic impulse was needed to achieve a fuller union of words and music along the lines of regular bar-rhythm in which the whole art was advancing. The dramatic influence had been long delayed in English music, and the masques, from those of Ben Jonson to 'Comus', had done little or nothing to make it felt, because in them the play proceeded on its own lines; the songs were a mere inset taking no part in its action. The musician who wrote for such masques had no inducement to identify himself with the characters of the play, to make them speak in person through his music, as Monteverdi had made his Orpheus speak. In the middle of the seventeenth century Christopher Sympson, author of *The Division Viol*, could still speak of 'the dramatic or recitative music; which, as yet, is something a stranger to us, here, in England'.

When the 'representative style' did come it grew naturally out of Lawes's way of setting metrical words in strict time, not out of a copy of the free declamation of the Italian and French operas. Curiously enough, it made its appearance most decisively during the decade of Puritan rule between the execution of the first King Charles and the Restoration of the second.

The Puritans offered no wholesale opposition to the arts. They objected to church music because they objected to the Church, and to stage plays because they were an incitement to immorality. Oliver Cromwell was himself a musical man, so musical that he stole the organ from Magdalen College Chapel and had it erected at Hampton Court for his artistic delectation. Playford's *Dancing Master* was published in 1650 and ran through several editions during the Puritan decade. Concerted music for viols succeeded in popularity to the position which madrigal singing had formerly held in domestic music, and Sympson's *Division Viol* took the place of Morley's *Plaine and Easie Introduction*.

Writing at the end of the century, Henry Purcell

Towards English Opera

looked back to the curious entertainment held at Rutland House in May 1656 as 'the first Opera we ever had in England', and described it as a 'perfect Opera', because it was sung throughout. Its music is lost, but we know that its title was 'The Siege of Rhodes', that its music was composed by five men, Henry Lawes himself, Cook, who afterwards became Charles II's first choirmaster in the re-established Chapel Royal, Matthew Locke, and two others, Colman and Hudson, of less importance. No doubt it was a curious hotchpotch, but it served to evade the prohibition of stage plays by introducing the play under cover of a musical entertainment. Thus opera entered England by the back door, not because anybody wanted opera but because some people disapproved of the 'legitimate' theatre. It has been going in and out of the back door ever since.

Matthew Locke is the most interesting figure in this group of composers. He was destined to fight harder for English opera than any other man, and to go far to solve this problem of English declamatory song. In collaboration with Christopher Gibbons, the son of Orlando, he produced in London, on the eve of the Restoration of the Monarchy (1659),[1] the music to a masque written by James Shirley, in which there are scenes of such genuinely dramatic power that it may be pointed to as representing the birth of English opera. It was called 'Cupid and Death'.[2] The most significant thing about 'Cupid and Death' is that it is a comic piece. This separates it at once from the earlier

[1] It appears to have been given privately for the entertainment of the Portuguese Ambassador, six years before in May, 1653.
[2] 'Cupid and Death' was revived by the Glastonbury Players in 1919 and given at Glastonbury in a version prepared from the original by E. J. Dent, which still remains unpublished. Professor Dent kindly allowed me to make a copy from his manuscript from which 'Nature's Song', with his pianoforte accompaniment, was sung at these lectures. The examples quoted here have been transcribed from Locke's own manuscript in the British Museum.

classical and allegorical masques designed more for the entertainment of the amateur performers than for presentation to a mixed audience. In it Shirley hit on and developed an idea of topsy-turvydom of the kind which more than two hundred years later made the success of the Savoy Operas. Cupid and Death meet at an Inn, and with the help of a comic waiter they dine well and both are put to bed. While they are lying in a drunken slumber the waiter changes their weapons so that in the morning Cupid goes off armed with the shafts of Death and Death carries the darts of Cupid. This Gilbertian notion is carried to its logical conclusion when Cupid, seeing some nice young couples gently flirting, shoots at them with fatal results, and Death, seeing some old folk, thinks to dispatch them and finds that his shaft rejuvenates them. They begin to dance and make love to one another. While a good deal of the dialogue is spoken and diversified with songs and dances written partly by Locke and partly by Gibbons, this scene, the clue of the whole piece, is set to continuous music by Locke in a long scena sung by Nature, who warns her children to fly from the 'frantic' Cupid. The style can be fully realized only when the whole song is sung, but the two entrances which interrupt it are here quoted for illustration:

The bass is Locke's way of indicating roughly, according to the careless fashion of the time, the harmonies on which the harpsichordist was to found his accompaniment. The precise art of the lute with its tablature has given way to this haphazard method. But it is the declamation which is all important. It looks like recitative, but the essential thing to notice is that its eloquence depends entirely on its being sung in strict time. This it has in common with Lawes's songs. But the blank verse is not set metrically. Sing these passages through, beating an inflexible four in a bar, and you get an exact musical counterpart of an intelligent and dramatic reading of the lines. This is the rule which every one who wants to sing Locke or Purcell (who founded his style on Locke) must master at the outset; it is constantly ignored by those brought up either on the opera recitative of the Italians or the narrative recitative of Bach. The chief source of expression is in the time values of the notes. Note, for example, the diminishing energy of the phrase to which the Lover's words are set and the accentuation of the line 'Nature grows stiff with horror of this spectacle'. One finds here rhythmic groups created by the words in just the way that Merbecke began to indicate them a hundred years earlier. 'Spectacle', indeed, is equivalent to Merbecke's 'Visible and invisible' (cf. p. 31).

Locke, moreover, uses harmony to reinforce this rhythmic expression. The change in the old people is made vivid by the grave flat harmonies of 'the heavy burden of their lives', followed by the brilliant chord of G major. Such things are inherent in the attempt to represent in music a scene not contemplated or described but actually present to the senses. They are of the essence of dramatic music. Once more in Locke the man and the movement came together. The reaction from Puritanism placed the theatre in the forefront of the social life of London, and in him was found a man ready to unite the English language and the English song in its service. He was ready to create the English opera. He nearly did it, but not quite. We shall see presently why Locke, like Merbecke, was one of the might-have-beens.

CHAPTER V
HENRY PURCELL—LIFE AND TIMES

SO far I have attempted to establish the fact that in that emergence of the vernacular as the vehicle for the development of music, which was an outcome of the Renaissance, the several nations most affected by it took their own courses in accordance with the principles of their languages and the dictates of temperament. The Italians, most clear sighted and originative, went straight for their mark and achieved it conclusively through the *stile rappresentativo* which produced a great form of art, the Opera, to which they have remained singularly faithful ever since. Their acquirement was passed to the French and, at the court of Louis Quatorze, a composer of Italian origin, Jean Baptiste Lully, moulded the general principle in conformity with the just declamation of the French language and with French ideals of dramatic form and expression. Lully, in fact, by the foundation of the Académie Royale de Musique, the institution still represented by the Paris Opéra, was given ample opportunity to do for France what his contemporary, Matthew Locke, was showing himself ready to do for England. But the same opportunity did not come to the Englishman.

The Germans moved as directly towards their goal as the Italians did to theirs, but it was a very different goal. Luther set it up with the invention of the Protestant chorale round which the contemplative cantata and the Passion oratorio gradually crystallized. German vocal music, founded on the local form of the Christian religion, remained provincial in character up to and including the work of its master, J. S. Bach. The dramatic idea was to permeate it at a much later date.

Meanwhile the English tendency to compromise on matters of principle and to be careless in matters of art produced these sporadic and apparently disconnected efforts which we have been studying. I have tried to show you that in them a certain sequence can be traced, and that John Merbecke, Thomas Weelkes, Orlando Gibbons, John Dowland, Henry Lawes, and Matthew Locke all mark definite stages in the difficult process of training the language and the art of music to run together in double harness. Their accomplishments were lightly regarded. Merbecke's Prayer Book was thrown on the scrap-heap as soon as the Protestant party got a little more political power; Weelkes and Gibbons were soon outmoded, and I have suggested that the madrigal was hurried towards its decay by incompetent performance.

Dowland's style of song-writing was certainly too fine a thing for rough and ready amateur performance; Lawes's type was too mechanical a thing to outlive its immediate purpose in the masque. Locke found the time ripe for English opera and formed a style for it perfectly suited to linguistic needs, as Monteverdi's had been to the Italian needs. Henry Purcell came to mould that style into the finished product. The English people blew hot and cold towards him and it, as they had towards all his predecessors.

We know very little personally about the man who, until the recent revival of the Elizabethans began, was customarily spoken of as the greatest of English composers, and I have nothing here to relate of the facts of his life which may not be found concisely stated in any biographical dictionary.[1] But it is necessary to recall some of those facts in order to see him in his environment, and to discover from them how it happened that Purcell was so exactly fitted to do the particular work he did do, what his claims to greatness are, why they were so fully recognized by his contemporaries, and why his work was so neglected after his death. All the records agree in attesting the honour paid to Purcell during his short life.

[1] While this book was in the press *Henry Purcell* by Dennis Arundell, a short but reliable life, was published by the Oxford University Press.

Henry Purcell—Life and Times

He was born presumably at Westminster, 1658–9, and no closer reckoning of his birth is obtainable than that which the monument to him in Westminster Abbey affords by the statement that he died on 21 Nov. 1695 in the thirty-seventh year of his age. His father, also Henry Purcell, was a singing man at Westminster and Pepys's *Diary* gives a glimpse of him as a 'Master of Musique' whose acquaintance Pepys, insatiable music-lover that he was, evidently valued. The father died, however, while the younger Henry was still a small child and the latter was left to the care of an uncle, Thomas Purcell, who, being a Gentleman of the Chapel Royal, newly re-established for Charles II with Captain Cooke as 'Master of the Children', was able to use his influence to get the boy into the choir at an early age. The Chapel Royal then became his home and his school. There he remained until several years after the breaking of his voice and until he emerged from it to enter on the diverse musical life of London and soon to succeed to the important post of organist at Westminster Abbey.

It was a disturbed and rapidly changing city in which the boy was brought up and from which he gathered his first and indeed his only impressions of the world. We have no positive knowledge, indeed, that Purcell ever left London, though we may suppose that he did in fact make such excursions out of it as a busy man of his proclivities would be likely to make; to Windsor to present and perform the odes which he wrote for royal occasions, or to a country cathedral to play on a new organ built by his friend 'Father Smith'. Every record that we have of Purcell, however, shows him engaged in some activity in London or Westminster. He may for all we know have never gone outside the four-mile radius from Charing Cross.

The London of his early youth was a place in which old institutions were being hastily rehabilitated and society was rushing feverishly to obliterate the traces of the late irregular government miscalled a Commonwealth. The King had come into his own again and the Church with him. His palace at Whitehall was refurbished to receive him, and Smith's first job was to build an organ for its banqueting hall. The King's 'Chapel' was formed, and Captain Cooke busied himself in creating a choir for it. The liturgy of the Church of England had been banned for some ten years or more; choir books had been destroyed, organs torn down. There was plenty of work for the enterprising organ-builder. Every Cathedral Church in the country, with the Collegiate Chapels of Oxford and Cambridge, was anxious to recreate its clerical and musical establishment and resume its daily services. Places were filled more with the purpose of rewarding loyalty to the Crown, real or supposed, than according to the fitness of the individual. The King had not enough places to give, especially since he wanted a good many of those available for the friends of his exile. He soon repented of having placed the music of his Chapel in the hands of the worthy Cooke, who, however, had shown undoubted skill in collecting a choir of clever 'children', but who made them sing the service according to what he remembered of the old English tradition. Pelham Humfrey, John Blow, and Michael Wise, all of them destined later to attain some distinction as composers, were among the first group of choristers; Purcell was one of the second relay. Pepys soon noted that the King was 'a little musical' since he beat time with his hand through the anthem. He was musical enough to be bored by his painstaking English choir. He began to gather French musicians around him for his private entertainment. The story of how he caused Pelham Humfrey to be picked out as the brightest of the boys and sent to France to study under Lully, his expenses being defrayed from the 'Secret Service fund', has been often told. Too much has been made of it as regards its effect on English music in general, and Purcell in particular, as I shall try presently to

Henry Purcell—Life and Times

show you. We need only note it here as a symptom of that restless search for entertainment and novelty which we can recognize and in a measure sympathize with to-day, as belonging inevitably to a post-war period. There was a reaction not only from the late Puritan government but from the Civil War behind it and from the period of strenuous political thinking behind that. Purcell was born into a world which wanted to be amused.

William Davenant, who had projected those tentative musico-dramatic entertainments described at the end of the last chapter, quickly opened a theatre in Lincoln's Inn Fields (1662); Thomas Killigrew in the following year opened another in Drury Lane, the original of the present theatre there, and for ten years or so two theatrical companies were catering for the amusement of the court and the town. Both were situated in outlying parts of the town, and both therefore escaped the fire of 1666 which swept the City of London from east to west and destroyed practically all its ancient landmarks, including St. Paul's Cathedral. With the city itself a mass of charred ruins, social life naturally moved westward; the houses of noblemen along the north bank of the Thames were already beginning to form a link between London proper and Westminster, where the King's court was in residence, and from the first years of the Restoration therefore begins that process by which Charing Cross became in later times the virtual centre of London. The river was the natural highway connecting London and Westminster, and it provided the safest and speediest means of locomotion between them. In 1671 Sir William Davenant, knighted for his services, brought his company of players from Lincoln's Inn Fields to the more commodious new theatre built in Dorset Garden just east of the Temple, which could be readily reached by water.

It was here that experiments in more elaborate

musical productions were made, Matthew Locke leading off by writing some music to an altered version of Shakespeare's *Macbeth*.[1] *The Tempest*, 'made into an Opera' by Thomas Shadwell, followed and Matthew Locke's instrumental music to *The Tempest* was subsequently published by him together with his music to another production, *Psyché*, under the title of 'The English Opera'.

This 'making into an opera' of Shakespearian and other plays was a thing very different from anything which we should describe by that name. No attempt was made to set the main action of the play to music. The taste of Restoration audiences reverted to the masques of the first Caroline era with their lavish use of scenic display, costumes, dancing, and music. The opera is best described as the masque professionalized, for it was now the King's players and musicians who provided the entertainment for the delectation of the court, who looked on and marvelled at the spectacle. The thing was more like the modern pantomime of Drury Lane than the opera of Covent Garden. The original plays were re-written, additional characters were added to them, the poetry of Shakespeare's lines was sacrificed to meretricious effects of every kind. Supernatural scenes, the witches of *Macbeth*, the fairies and sprites controlled by Prospero in *The Tempest*, were considered the only appropriate ones for music. They were expanded into something which would make an effective fragment of opera tacked on to the spoken dialogue of the other characters. Thus much opportunity Locke, and after him Purcell, had for the development of their art of declamatory song; no more. The musician was a secondary element in the scheme, of con-

---

[1] Whether this is the well-known Macbeth music edited with Locke's name by Boyce in the eighteenth century is uncertain. That music has been also ascribed to Purcell, but for this there is no good authority. Pelham Humfrey also wrote some music for *Macbeth* which was given in more than one version.

Henry Purcell—Life and Times

siderably less importance to the audience than the machinist. 'Machines' were indeed a first consideration in this 'Opera'. Witches must fly up, gods descend to earth, astonishing transformations be effected. The Dorset Garden theatre was designed for the better employment of machines in these effects of magic and mystery. Operas were not called by the names of their musical composers. In some cases we have no very certain knowledge as to who actually provided the music for a given production.

Such were the institutions of the exciting and perturbing city from which Purcell gained the impressions on which his own art was to be founded. We know nothing of his actual employment during his Chapel Royal days. There is a story that he composed music for an 'Address of the Children of the Chapel Royal to the King' in 1670, when he would have been about twelve years old, but in view of the fact that later historians have ascribed every conceivable and inconceivable achievement to Purcell's youth, as though his greatness depended on their proof of his precocity, we need place no reliance on it. All we do know from his subsequent work is that Cooke must have grounded him well in the old English counterpoint, that his musical knowledge must have been gained largely in his daily experience of singing the service, and that either Cooke or another made him a good harpsichord and organ player.

Cooke died and was succeeded in his post of 'Master of the Children' in 1672 by Pelham Humfrey, who, we know from a famous entry of Pepys, had returned from France 'a regular monsieur' full of conceit and puppyish affectation, though Pepys, for all his disgust at his manners, had to admit him to be a good musician. Purcell, therefore, at the age of fourteen came directly under Humfrey's tutorship. It does not follow that he imbibed any of Humfrey's ideas, indeed a passage in his preface to his 'Sonnatas of three Parts', written years later and after Humfrey's death, is either a recantation of those ideas or an acknowledgement that he had always been in revolt against them. It suggests that he may have begun 'to loathe the levity and balladry of our neighbours' from the time that Pelham Humfrey became his master and prated of French music and French ways to the disparagement of all things English.

The one thing which it seems likely that Humfrey did for him was to enable him to find his way to Dorset Garden theatre. Cooke, one suspects, would have been less likely to send his choir-boys there. Again we are left to conjecture, but the coincidence of Humfrey's appointment to the Chapel Royal with the opening of the theatre and the fashionable craze for pseudo-opera, in the provision of which Humfrey certainly took a share, suggests that Humfrey may have brought the boy into contact with theatrical life. If so, it is something for which he deserves the thanks of posterity, for Purcell's instinct for the theatre, ripened by early experience, is the salient characteristic of his maturity.

Even here, however, it was Locke who exerted the more direct influence on Purcell. If Humfrey took or sent Purcell to the theatre it was Locke's art that he admired when he got there, and Locke, be it remembered, knew and cared little or nothing about the Lullian style of theatre music which Humfrey had imbibed and which he belauded simply because it was foreign and therefore 'the latest thing'. We have seen Locke evolving an English type of declamatory song in accordance with the needs of the language in the years before the King had come back bringing the French fashions with him, and the pieces which Locke wrote for the Dorset Garden theatre were a continuation of what he had begun to do in 'Cupid and Death'.

Locke had a sturdy belief in his country's art and a healthy confidence in his own powers. His controversial writings show a truculent attitude towards opponents and an acrimonious manner of debate. He wrote a preface to his publication of 'The English Opera', mentioned above, which has historical importance as the first of the many fruitless arguments in favour of English opera which have been issued by musical enthusiasts of successive generations down to the present day. In it he attempted to answer each objection likely to be advanced by those who asserted the superiority of the Italian style. His argument, however, fell on deaf ears like all its successors, and for the same reason; there were not enough people who really cared about the matter. Further, the preface shows Locke's spirit, for in it he dilates on what had been done to create an English opera and roundly declares that he had done most of it, which was quite true.

Locke was an old friend of Purcell's father, and the adoration of Purcell's youth, his own great exemplar. It seems that for a few years after Purcell's voice broke, when consequently he ceased to be an active member of the choir, he was kept on at the Chapel Royal and that he then studied composition with John Blow, who was about ten years older than himself, and who had succeeded to the post of organist at Westminster Abbey.

No doubt many of his earlier essays in composition were in the form of church anthems, which were the staple of all English music as the only thing which could be certain of gaining an immediate and constant performance. But we know that he had also begun song-writing, for one or two of his songs appeared in the two volumes of 'Choice Ayres' which John Playford issued and are therefore his first publications.

Most remarkable among them is an 'Elegy on the Death of Matthew Locke'[1] (1677), which, if there were no other evidence, would prove his discipleship. Whether the verses are written by Purcell himself or by some poetaster of the day, they are in themselves very

[1] Re-published in *Seventeen Songs, by Purcell* (Novello, 1927), with pianoforte accompaniment arranged by Arthur Somervell.

illuminating, because they do much more than bestow merely conventional laudation on the dead.

They are worth quotation:

(*Declamatory. Common time*)

> What hope for us remains now he is gone?
> He that knew all the pow'rs of numbers, flown
> Alas! too soon; ev'n he whose skilful harmony
> Had charms for all the ills that we endure,
> And could apply a certain cure.
> From pointed griefs he'd take the pain away,
> Ev'n ill nature did his lyre obey,
> And in kind thoughts his artful hand repay.
> His lays to anger and to war could move,
> Then calm the tempest they had rais'd with love,
> And with soft sounds to gentle thoughts incline,
> No passion reign'd where he did not combine.
> He knew such mystic touches that in death
> Could cure the fear; or stop the parting breath
> And if to die had been his fear or life his care,
> He with his lyre could call and could unite
> His spirits to the fight, and vanquish Death
> In his own field of night.

(*Lyrical. Triple time*)

> Pleased with some powerful Hallelujah, he
> Wrapped in the joys of his own harmony
> Sung on, and flew up to the Deity.

It is the first line which from its personal character suggests that the words may be by Purcell, for the 'us' must surely mean the younger artists whom Locke had inspired with his ideals. In the second line the reference to 'the pow'rs of numbers' emphasizes that capacity for dealing with words in song which Locke in fact passed on to Purcell, while there seems a covert reference to Locke's love of polemical controversy in the suggestion that 'ill nature' itself must yield to the power of his music. Those who know Locke's instrumental music to *The Tempest*, which contains what we should now call a short symphonic poem for strings descriptive of the tempest raised by Prospero and allayed at the urgent instance of Miranda, will recognize the allu-

Henry Purcell—Life and Times 79

sion of the tenth line, and that to Locke's church music (with the treatment of the word 'Hallelujah' in the rhythm characteristic of the Restoration composers) is obvious.

In short, the verses are written by some one to whom Locke's music was daily bread and Purcell's music to it is equally the product of Locke's style. It is the homage of a pupil to his master. It deserves to be studied as Purcell's starting-point in composition. As an instance of Purcell's declamatory treatment of words (observe that the whole moves perfectly in strict time[1] like the scena of 'Cupid and Death'), one phrase may here be quoted:

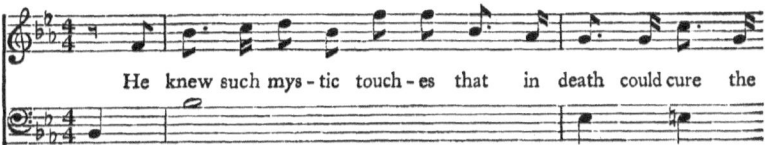

Note the skill with which the chromatic harmonies hurry on the declamation up to the word 'stop'.

Purcell was not long in getting into the saddle of his creative work, and that was well, for he had not long time in which to work. At the age of twenty-one or thereabouts he took up his duties as organist of Westminster Abbey in place of his former teacher, John Blow, who inexplicably retired before him to return there at his death. From 1680 up to 1695, when he died, the fifteen years of working life were filled full to overflowing. It was in 1680 that he first wrote theatre music for 'Theodosus, or the force of Love', a play which

[1] The modern editor has unfortunately given the wrong suggestion to singers by printing *quasi recit.* at the beginning of the song.

was rendered lucrative to the company according to Downes by the perfect performance and the success of Purcell's music; 'the Court, especially the ladies by their daily charming preference for it, gave it great encouragement'.[1]

With Locke and Humfrey both dead Purcell became the musical darling of the town. Every post was open to him, every music making of church or theatre, and soon of the concert-room, required something from him and would have been incomplete without him. The year 1680 shows him launching out in all directions. It is also the year of his first royal ode, 'Welcome, Vice Regent', to celebrate the King's return from Windsor. In the summer months he settled down to explore the possibilities of pure instrumental music, writing those fantasies[2] for strings in a varying number of parts which are his first essay in that direction, and also practically the last of the long line of 'Fancies' which the old English composers had evolved from the vocal madrigal style (cf. p. 4).

His imaginative enterprise was now fully awakened, and the fantasies bear the stamp of his personality in innumerable melodic and harmonic details. But they were evidently undertaken primarily as exercises. He never published them. He was soon too busy to indulge in composition for its own sake; he had to supply occasions. A year or two later he added the organistship of the Chapel Royal to that of the Abbey. The King's death in 1685 brought the need for coronation music for James II, and the subsequent revolution gave him another coronation, that of William and Mary, to provide for within his short term of office. Purcell turned out the required 'Welcome Odes' for every royal occasion regardless of changing times and the rapid rise and

[1] *Roscius Anglicanus*, a record of the plays produced, made at a later date from recollection, by John Downes, the prompter at the theatre.

[2] Published by Curwen for the first time in 1926, edited by Philip Heseltine.

Henry Purcell—Life and Times

fall of dynasties. Some of them are obviously written with his left hand, so to speak, but together they attest his extraordinary fertility of invention, his almost Schubert-like gift of melody, and above all his unerring instinct for the placing of words in the music.

A more fruitful institution than the royal odes was the celebration of St. Cecilia's Day (22 Nov.), which was made the occasion for a musical festival in London consisting of a church service and a performance in one of the City Companies' halls. Purcell began his active co-operation in this in 1683, when he produced three choral odes, one of them to a Latin text; he carried it farther in 1692 with the most famous of his odes, the magnificent 'Hail, bright Cecilia', and completed it with the great 'Te Deum' and 'Jubilate' in D for choir and orchestra (1694), which was destined to become one of the works on which the Three Choirs Festival was founded. He died on the eve of the festival of 1695.

Another significant event of 1683 is his first independent publication on a large scale, no less an enterprise than twelve Sonatas for two violins, string bass (violoncello or bass viol), and harpsichord (figured bass) under the title of 'Sonnatas of three Parts'. This was the occasion for the preface in which he exhorted his countrymen to 'loathe the levity and balladry of our neighbours' and declared his desire to bring the 'seriousness and gravity' of the Italian style into vogue. On that point something must be said later; here I only refer to the preface for the light which it throws on Purcell's character. Its English is slipshod; its tone happy-go-lucky, save for that moment in which, remembering the insufferable Humfrey, he allows himself a little spurt of venom against the French fashions. He is not proud of himself; unlike his admired Matthew Locke, he does not say that he has done more than any other; on the contrary he suggests that there are 'pens and artists of more eminent abilities, much better qualified for the employment than his or himself', not necessarily because he really thinks so, but because there may be, and anyhow courtesy is pleasanter than rudeness. He confesses his ignorance of the Italian language, deplores the 'unhappiness of his education' without deeply regretting it, like a thorough Englishman, and proceeds to explain a little incorrectly the Italian terms used in the music. Finally, he hopes that his work will come into the hands of only those 'who carry musical souls about them' and adds his 'Vale'.

You see from this the sort of man he was; not a pioneer (who must always be something of a fanatic) to force his art on his fellows and make them honour it; not, on the other hand, a pedant fussy over small things and nervously anxious to show himself in the right. His was a genial nature, one which accepted circumstances, generally made the best of them, but was just too indolent to change them radically. So he did the work which came to him, joined some of his best music to the fulsome futilities of the court poets, wrote brilliant songs and dances for play after play, enlarged the musical scenes of the pseudo-opera into such masterpieces as the Masque in *Diocletian* and the fourth act of *The Fairy Queen*, but never brought a complete opera on to the professional stage.

Dido and Aeneas shows that his failure in this respect was not from any lack of clear perception on his part of what real opera should be. It is, in fact, a little masterpiece of music-drama equal to anything produced by continental composers of the seventeenth century and far surpassing the majority of them. The opportunity for it came through a certain Josiah Priest who was ballet-master at Dorset Garden, and also the proprietor of a select finishing school for young ladies at Chelsea. Dancing and deportment with music were prominent among the accomplishments which formed the education of the young ladies, and Priest invited Purcell to provide an entertainment in which they could show their proficiency. Nahum Tate wrote a little play in three acts on the courtship of Dido by Aeneas, their separation accomplished by malevolent witches and the broken-hearted death of the heroine; a mixture of classical mythology with the customary magical paraphernalia of the Restoration stage, which gave plenty of scope for characterization in the music and for the song and dance of the young ladies. Purcell set it mostly for treble voices, though Aeneas (a tenor) and the choral tenor and bass parts were probably undertaken by singers from the Opera; a prologue was spoken before it by Lady Dorothy Burk,[1] but from the overture to the final chorus the music was continuous throughout each act.

Save for the form of the concise overture (a slow movement followed by a quick fugal one) there is not a trace of French influence in the music of *Dido and Aeneas*. The dialogue is all written in that strict-time declamation which Purcell had inherited from Locke as belonging to the English language. The dialogues lead straight into short but always expressive airs, three of which are in the form of the song on a 'ground-bass' which Purcell had made his own. Duets, choruses, and even dance-tunes are all strikingly original in form, all as Byrd said of his madrigals 'framed to the life of the words', not recognizable as belonging to any established types. The courtly measures of Dido's attendants, the wicked laughter of the witches, the bluff jollity of Aeneas's sailors, are alike perfectly suggested and effectively contrasted in the music, and while minor characters, incidents, and scenic accessories (the hunting horns in the distance, the menace of the storm, &c.) are aptly touched in, the emotions of the chief characters are always the composer's principal concern and are kept well in the foreground of his musical picture.

[1] It was by tracing out the history of this young lady that Barclay Squire was able to determine the date of production as not earlier than 1688.

Dido is a real woman. Nahum Tate gave Purcell the chance to make her so, but, from her heartsearchings before Aeneas appears to her lament after he has gone, it is Purcell's art which clothes with reality what in the words alone was merely the expression of correct sentiment.

It is the turn of the phrase which gives the personal feeling here; in the sighs on chromatically rising notes and the emphasis of the minim on 'him' she betrays her secret. Other feminine attributes are slyly suggested when Aeneas boasts of his prowess as a hunter and she with a sidelong glance at the sky (an upward turning phrase) remarks that it is going to rain, and again, when Aeneas is pompous about his departure and she fairly snaps his head off, mimicking his phrase and turning it to her own ends.

In such human characteristics Purcell sweeps away the artificialities of the Restoration stage. Gods and goddesses, witches, nymphs, and fairies, symbolical figures representing the seasons of the year, night and day, light and darkness, all these were the common stock of the masque and of the pseudo-opera of Dorset Garden.

For the schoolgirls at Chelsea he drew a heroine who is more than half a schoolgirl herself, with a court of schoolgirls round her; Dido ready to fall in love yet half afraid, Belinda and the others egging her on with coaxing admiration, and singing (cf. example on p. 117)

> Fear no danger to pursue,
> The hero loves as well as you,

in melody of a purely virginal quality. Dido's last song, 'When I am laid in earth', is too well known to require any comment except that it should not be divorced, as its concert performance too often necessitates, from the final chorus 'With drooping wings, ye cupids come'. This is not only one of the most simply appealing things in the whole range of vocal music but it is one of the very few operatic finales which touch sublimity because it is entirely in keeping with what has gone before it. No need here for the apotheosis, the grand *Chaconne* or the sumptuous stage displays which have spoilt so many operatic endings.

Purcell could afford to be natural and he was, just as Bach was in the finales to his Passion Music. I know of nothing else to which it may be fitly compared. In this one work Purcell was able to shake himself free of all the trammels of his time. His genius appears unspotted by the world.

CHAPTER VI
PURCELL TO-DAY

TWO hundred years after Henry Purcell's death he was remembered chiefly by a few anthems sung in English cathedrals with decreasing frequency on weekdays, when no one but a Dean, a Canon in residence, and a few ladies whose piety might be supposed to be proof against boredom, were likely to hear the performance. It was as well that they were not submitted to larger or more discriminating audiences, for the average lay-clerk's rendering of the 'Verses' (passages for one or more solo voices) was the most deplorably unintelligent thing that the witlessness of man ever conceived, and the effect of those anthems was dismal.

This did not much matter to the clerics and pious ladies who heard them, but nevertheless it created a very wrong impression of Purcell, and one still current to-day. As with Purcell himself and his contemporaries, so now, many of the most able musical minds in this country have begun life as choir-boys, have been articled as pupils to cathedral organists and have held such positions themselves. If you question them narrowly you will find that they hold a rather poor opinion of Purcell. I have been privileged to number many such among my friends; I have scarcely known one among them who cared for Purcell as I do. Most of them tolerate him as a useful adjunct of daily services; a few of the bolder spirits will openly declare that his reputation has been inflated by the historians and critics from Burney onwards, and that after all his music is scrappy and ephemeral. Some will compare his work disadvantageously with the noble polyphony of the Elizabethans, and condemn him as frivolous. It may seem strange that the lay-clerk's drone of 'O sing unto the Lord' should have earned him that epithet, but I have heard it used of that very anthem.

Now ex-choir-boys and cathedral organists do not remain inside their cathedrals performing services and anthems before Deans and pious ladies. They go out into the world; they head our musical colleges, hold university professorships, and in general lead the musical education of the country. It becomes, therefore, a serious matter for the community at large if their minds have been so warped at an early age towards one of the great figures in music, let alone native music, that they cannot even persuade themselves to acquire a working knowledge of his art and have no desire to encourage others to do so.

No wonder that Purcell remains under a cloud in popular estimation, and that his advocates are apt to be set down as faddists and special pleaders. Nothing is more difficult to eradicate than a 'complex' of this sort, and probably our cathedral-trained musicians will never be able to think of Purcell as anything but the purveyor of a quantity of tedious church music, who occasionally, in a flash of inspiration, wrote a beautiful song like 'When I am laid in earth' or the 'Evening hymn'. Moreover, they will imbue a whole younger generation of music-lovers with that view, so that the chance of Purcell once more taking his rightful place at the head of our musical classics seems remote. I hope, however, that I have left no doubt in your minds that the whole of that development of the English language in song in which great men like Byrd, Weelkes, and Dowland, and small men like Merbecke, Campian, and Lawes, all shared, led up to Purcell and was crowned by him.

Further, I suggest that the halting condition of music in England after his death was primarily due to the fact that his generation, despite the admiration showered on him, had refused to learn his lesson, partly no doubt because he had not the vigorous temperament to enforce it. A question before us is whether it can ever be learnt now.

One of the many disadvantages under which Purcell's

music labours now is that it is practically impossible to put most of his work in anything like its own setting, since all of it, except perhaps the concerted chamber music for strings, was devised for a setting which belonged peculiarly to his time. At first sight that may not seem to be true of his church music. Westminster Abbey still stands; the *Book of Common Prayer* of 1662 has remained continually in use, and at the present moment the question of whether the Church desires to alter or supplement it in any particular is being debated. Surely, it may be argued, if Purcell's church music was good then it is good now, and the taste of the experts, the cathedral organists, and others, who think poorly of it, is probably sound. To this there are two answers. One is that the Anglican Church and its services of 1927 is by no means the same thing as that of two hundred and fifty years before, despite the survival of its buildings and the continuity of its liturgy; the other, what I have already hinted, that Purcell's anthems are not in fact performed according to anything like his original intention. Were he to hear them as they are sung it is even possible that he would not recognize them for his own compositions.

The Church of the second Caroline era was separated from that of the first by a gulf far wider than that created by the change from Latin to English a hundred years before. Orlando Gibbons could write music for the Church of Archbishop Laud which differed little in form and not at all in spirit from that which Taverner had provided for Cardinal Wolsey's college. Through all the changes of doctrine and ritual which separated them there had remained a general agreement as to what characteristics in music were desirable as adjuncts to church worship. Taverner and Gibbons could approach their task from the same point of view. Roughly we may describe it as the survival of the monastic ideal in the contemplation of Divine Mysteries, whether the Mysteries were found in the Mass or the Bible.

Purcell To-day

Purcell was born after the Puritans had swept away mystery; the Restoration Church was powerless to restore it. You have only to read Samuel Pepys to realize that its services were regarded as a discreet entertainment, participation in which was a sign of loyalty to the Crown and the Constitution, rather than to any more spiritual authority. Charles II's commission to Humfrey was virtually to brighten up church music by giving it some of the more lively flavour of what he had enjoyed at the court of Versailles. Purcell was brought up in this atmosphere; he never knew any other, save that during his life the spiritual wickedness in high places of the second Stuart monarchy changed to the smug respectability of the 'Protestant succession', which fastened on the Church of England under William and Mary a very different protestantism from the keen-edged sword of the Lord which the Puritan had carried through the land a generation earlier.

Purcell, a child of the Restoration with his heart in the theatre, had to make his living in this disillusioned and unmystic Church. What could he do? He did the best that any artist can do; he was at all times frankly and unashamedly himself. He pretended to no piety which was unreal to him. He searched the Psalms and the Prophets for his anthem texts. In the former especially he found congenial material. His music dramatized the emotions of the Psalmist. If he sang 'Praise the Lord, O my Soul' his strains reflected an exultant physical joy, a sense of well-being. If he sang 'Thy thoughts are very deep' he conjured up a picture of Divine omniscience, and when he declared 'A fool doth not well consider this', a note of scorn at the human frailty came naturally into his declamation. He had no idea of glossing over his feelings or of toning his voice to conform with the proprieties of clerical phraseology. 'Hallelujah' was to him a good rhythmical word with which he could round off an anthem with a vivid scherzo-like movement, almost a dance, of the kind which would bring down the curtain effectively in the theatre. Generally that curtain fell after he had touched some emotion of joy or sorrow, fear, awe or wonder, with the directness of the true dramatist.

His 'verse' anthems are for the most part devised in a series of short movements rapidly changing their style in accordance with the suggestions of the words, and beginning with a well-planned instrumental movement for strings with organ, since in the Chapel Royal the co-operation of the King's violinists could be relied on. They are concise cantatas, not differing greatly in style from the 'Welcome Odes', except in their greater reliance on movements for combined men's solo voices (alto, tenor, and bass) which often take the place of the single-voiced declamation of the stage works.

To our ears this is almost always a rather unsatisfactory combination, but it was evidently admired in Purcell's day. He himself had inherited it from composers of an earlier generation, Locke, Christopher Gibbons, and Humfrey for example. In addition to the obvious fact that in cathedral choirs three lay-clerks are generally more than three times as bad as one, there is the difficulty of the male alto voice, which in the majority of cases is sung in 'falsetto' by a man whose natural voice is an inferior baritone. No doubt the falsetto alto was an institution of Purcell's day, but the true countertenor also existed and Purcell's own voice was of that kind. We know that he sang his own alto songs in the 'Ode on St. Cecilia's Day' (1692) and that his singing was much admired. At any rate it is quite clear that he never intended the inarticulate 'squawk' which we associate with the strange voice of the cathedral alto of to-day.

If we apply to Purcell's anthems, solo, concerted 'verse', and chorus alike, the same principle of singing in strict time at a pace convenient for the verbal articulation which we have seen to be the basis for the interpretation of both his and Locke's dramatic music, we find that they assume a wholly different character from that which conventional cathedral interpretation has given to them. Certainly they do not possess the statuesque beauty of the earlier church music, though there are plenty of passages which show that Purcell could command a massive polyphony when he wanted it, but they have none of the pose of devotionalism which gathered round the cathedral service when its routine had become firmly established. Sweep that pose away and sing them naturally and intelligently and they recover their freshness at once. Purcell's anthems may not have all the qualities we require of church music, but they have their own qualities in the expression of words by spontaneous melody of clear-cut rhythm supported by distinctive harmony.

That might be taken as a summary of Purcell's art, wherever he bestowed it, in church, theatre, or chamber. It is extraordinarily direct. The tune is always the thing that matters; the harmony is always ancillary to it, emphasizing the point of a melodic phrase. To a certain extent this is true of every good composer, but Purcell's restraint in the use of decoration of any kind makes his reliance on the melodic impulse the more conspicuous.

We customarily use the word 'tune' to mean something a little different from 'melody' or 'air', and we all know the difference without being able to define it. We can admit a piece of music to be melodious which is not a tune. Purcell's own declamatory passages are always melodious and yet are quite distinct from his tuneful songs. The Elegy on Matthew Locke begins as we have seen with declamatory melody and ends with a tune. Some musicians have defined tune as organized melody, and have shown successfully how a tune may be analysed into its component parts of balanced phrases; and conversely how it may be mechanically constructed by adding to an initial phrase others like it or vying with it and paying conscious regard to the twin principles of agreement and contrast. Certain formal composers, Handel, Haydn, and Beethoven, for example, lend themselves well to this kind of analysis, and in consequence it is no difficult matter for a well-instructed musician to make up a tune which might be mistaken by a careless listener for one of their less inspired movements (see Chapter VII).

Purcell's tunes defy this kind of analysis, and it would be a bold man who would attempt artificially to construct a Purcellian tune. It would be an interesting study to go through 'Orpheus Britannicus', the principal collection of his songs made during his life, and discover how many of them illustrate these principles of formal design. Certainly a great many of them do not. That which ends the Elegy on Locke is a typical case, in which a number of phrases quite unlike each other in outline succeed one another and yet are closely bound together by an inherent rhythm so that the total result perfectly achieves that coherence to which we instinctively give the name of tune. A tune is something which every person readily learns by heart, and therefore a tune is most readily made by an artful reflection of ideas, but genius may make a memorable tune with a minimum of repetition or even none at all, and no composer has done this more easily or more often than Purcell.

His instinct for tune-writing, mostly in connexion with words, tended to make his musical thought naturally measure itself to the length of a stanza. To us, accustomed to the arts of development which belong to the aria and the sonata, his movements, whether in the anthems, stage pieces, or odes, frequently seem rather short-breathed in consequence. It was probably some perception of a lack of constructive power in himself which made him seize with such eagerness on the Italian violin sonatas which came his way and take them for his models. What actually these sonatas were will probably always remain now a matter of some doubt, but that is not important. Italian violinists had come to court; Purcell had heard them, perhaps had borrowed their manuscripts. He may have obtained one or two published copies of early works by Vitali and others. He could have known nothing, except by hearsay, of Corelli, whose first book was only published in the same year as his own. He was struck by 'the seriousness and gravity of that sort of music' and no wonder, for the Italian sonata forms even in their primitive stage were designed to carry on a continuous *cantilena* without the aid of either insistent repetition or a restricted dance rhythm. They related the *cantilena* to contrasted key centres disposed in a logical order; they demanded concentration on the part of the listener to perceive the beauty produced by their simple pattern. They appealed, therefore, to the serious musician. In them Purcell saw the key to the development of a larger style than that of the 'curtain tune', the stage dance, and the unpremeditated lyrical song. He addressed himself to it with the results that we know in the twelve 'Sonnatas of three Parts' (published 1683) and the ten others which were not published till after his death.

He evidently set out to write his sonatas in as many different keys as were practicable considering the fixed intonation of the harpsichord which accompanied the strings, and which was not tuned in equal temperament. Up to this date English composers had explored very little that modulation from key to key which was to become the groundwork of all instrumental music of the sonata pattern. Their string fantasies were fashioned according to the old principles of modal counterpoint. Morley had even laid it down that leaving one key for another was the one thing which 'might never be suffered', and though this rule had gone the way which all academic prohibitions go sooner or later, yet modulation was no part of the design of the fantasie, and those which occurred were taken incidentally and without much perception of what they implied.

Purcell's twelve sonatas were written in twelve different keys, so as to give himself the opportunity of studying key-relationship from twelve different standpoints. There are six in minor and six in major keys, and the alternate arrangement of minor and major emphasizes his deliberate intention of studying the problem thoroughly. In this enterprise he was quite alone. We know that he could not speak Italian, so probably he could not converse about the theory of his art with the visiting violinists whom he so much admired. Indeed, living entirely in London and with only the Chapel Royal education behind him, he probably had no means of coming into contact with any of the more thinking minds of the Continent who were working on lines parallel to his. The average amateur of London might admire the results but was not likely to enter sympathetically into the finer points of technique by which they were attained. The crisp little dance-tunes of the theatre, some of which Purcell arranged for the harpsichord, probably served the popular taste better than the sonatas. In producing the latter Purcell had no incentive to industry beyond the pursuit of his own ideal, and no technical guidance other than the 'power of the Italian notes' in which, as he says, he could not be mistaken.

The result far surpassed the models, for Purcell's sonatas, embodying his gift of frank melody and his enterprise in chromatic harmony (at moments poignantly expressive) in a bold scheme of well-diversified movements, completely eclipse all others of their date. Corelli's Opus I, contemporary with Purcell's set, takes priority of importance only as an example of how to write for the strings and therefore as the basis of a great school of violin playing. Its musical matter does not compare in force and originality with Purcell's. It is, however, for its bearing on Purcell's subsequent developments in vocal music that we have here to take into account his experience of the Italian *cantilena*. His perception of the self-existent qualities of music was deepened by it and his style was broadened.

As illustration of this it is interesting to compare with the Elegy on Locke that 'On the death of Mr. John Playford', which was written ten years later (1687). The latter has nothing like the personal feeling which makes the Elegy on Locke so enlightening as a human document; Playford was a respected publisher by whose death, though relations were cordial, the composer would not be likely to be so deeply moved as by the death of a dearly loved master. The words by Nahum Tate are cast in the elaborate pastoral style in which shepherds are called on to 'lament for pious Theron's death', and mountains, fountains, dales, and vales are introduced because they provide an imagery as appropriate as their rhymes are convenient.

The paraphernalia of sorrow and consolation is conventional, but Purcell's music displays it with becoming dignity. His work might almost be described as a vocal sonata, for a short declamatory opening is succeeded by an intricate air on a ground bass and the two correspond to the *grave* and *canzona* of his sonata form. They, with a short stanza in the free *arioso* manner (triple time), are in the key of G minor. A complete change of mood comes with the lighter air 'Muses, bring your roses hither', which is also on a ground bass, but one of a more flowing character. The contrast is emphasized by a change of key, for this charming episode is in B flat major with cleverly suggested modulations to attendant keys achieved without alteration of the 'ground'. A return to the declamatory style and the more sombre mood is made simultaneously with a return to G minor, but a cheerful finale, its cheerfulness made appropriate by 'Theron's' fitness to join 'the sacred choir above', is made the more so by the bright key of G major in combination with the bold triple time measure. The voice part itself is very different from the simple style in which one note to a syllable of the words gives a precise accentual value both to the metre and the sense. Ornamental artifices are used to give graphic expression to such salient phrases as 'rending mountains', 'moan', 'endless fame', &c.

Purcell's handling of the ground bass, here and elsewhere, deserves attention. It was the most definite formal device which he ever used, and he resorted to it whenever he wanted to ensure a unified character to a movement of some length, leaving his voice part untrammelled by formal considerations. In this case that short figure dropping in fourths is repeated sixteen times, beginning alternately on the first and third of the bar. The vocal phrases overlap it, and often, as in the instance quoted, extend over two statements of the ground bass figure. Indeed, Purcell's rhythmic ingenuity is nowhere so well shown as in these ground bass movements, instrumental as well as vocal, in the way the regular phrase lengths created by the reiterations of the bass are crossed by the irregular phrases of the melody. Dido's first song 'Ah, Belinda' in *Dido and Aeneas* is a peculiarly subtle example of this.

The second ground bass of the Playford Elegy, 'Muses, bring your roses hither', gets rhythmic variety in the bass itself (a descending scale passage) by beginning it at different parts of the bar, so that the accents of the bar fall on different parts of the scale. It is by this means that, while the bass is always reiterating a scale of B flat, Purcell manages to give the effect of cadences modulating into both D minor and F major.

Occasionally Purcell would transpose the bass into a contrasted key for a middle section, returning to the original key as a sort of *reprise*. Dido's song mentioned above and the favourite 'Evening hymn' give instances of modulation to the dominant; 'Wondrous Machine' in the 'Ode on St. Cecilia's Day' has a modulation of the bass into the relative major.

It is unnecessary to attempt to analyse the exact nature of the several devices he employed in order to give musical form and outline to these more extended movements. The point to be emphasized is that in the few years of his maturity he made a distinct and conscious advance in style beyond the purely lyrical impulse of his tuneful songs and the dramatic aptness of his declamation, by applying to his vocal art some of the principles he had gleaned from the Italian instrumental sonatas, and that this advance was all in the direction of insistence on purely musical quality, that thinking in sound which is the *raison d'être* of the very name 'Sonata'.

It is natural enough that he should have carried the process farthest in the last and immeasurably the greatest of the odes which he wrote in praise of his beloved art. The words which Nicholas Brady gave him with which to celebrate St. Cecilia's Day 1692 may not be great poetry but they were inspiring to a man who, practically alone among his countrymen, was devoting his life to pressing forward towards new expressive possibilities in the world of sound.

> Hail, bright Cecilia,
> Fill every heart with love of thee and thy celestial art,

was the right text for Purcell to preach from. He summoned all his powers. He began with an overture, scored for what in his day was a large orchestra (two trumpets, drums, oboes, and strings) and which in general plan follows the lines of his usual sonata form. A short fanfare leads to a *canzona* in D major; there is an expressive slow movement in A minor and a brilliant and lighthearted finale, again in D. The several choruses, especially the opening one and the magnificent 'Soul of the World' in the middle of the work, are of the kind which are called 'Handelian' by musicians who have never known their Purcell and have forgotten most of their Handel. They unite massive choral effect with bold counterpoint (this was Purcell's inheritance from his English ancestors) and add to these resources that declamatory urgency which was Purcell's hall mark.

That change of accent which gives to the alto entry the effect of hastening to the attack would be meaningless without the bar accent. It is also a subtlety outside Handel's ken.

But it was in the solo numbers (including duets, trios,

Purcell To-day

and a quartet) that Purcell attempted to break new ground in musical style and in the handling of the words. Their manner is as different from that of his purely lyrical or tuneful songs as it is from the dramatic declamation of his theatre pieces. They are in a highly ornamented style after the manner of the *cantilena* of the Italian sonatas, but with the ornaments so directed as to dwell contemplatively on the implications of the words. They show Purcell getting away from the theatre far more thoroughly than he ever did in his church anthems. The mystery of music inspires him in a way which the mysteries of religion could not do.

The following extract is a fair sample of the prevailing texture:

You see at once that here the voices must not only feel the words but must phrase like violins. The problems which he sets them to solve are akin to those of Bach in the florid arias of the Passions and cantatas which in the middle of the last century were considered almost impracticable. Purcell's solos in the Ode are considered impracticable at the present day and consequently the work is scarcely ever performed as a whole. It has the additional difficulty that no less than three of the arias are written for the alto voice, that one duet is for alto and tenor, and that a trio and a quartet both demand first and second altos. By 'alto', as we have seen, Purcell meant the highest male voice, not the lowest female one. When a contralto sings these alto parts they lose their brilliance. The male alto is now almost extinct, except in the cathedral lay-clerk, who ought to be extinguished. The *Gentleman's Magazine* of 1692 tells us that Purcell sang the alto air "'tis nature's voice'[1] with 'incredible graces'. If he had a second alto as good as himself for the trio 'With that sublime celestial lay', it too must have created a wonderful effect.

The fact is that the 'Ode on St. Cecilia's Day' is not sung because our professional solo singers have no per-

---

[1] I had thought that this air was a case in which Purcell had overshot his mark and carried vocal ornament to the point of absurdity until a young Glasgow lady, a pupil of Mr. Roberton, sang it for me at these lectures. Her sense of rhythm overcame the disadvantage of the contralto quality and the song made a very powerful impression (see list of illustrations).

ception of the qualities of interpretation which it calls for. On the few occasions when it has been given in public it has been regarded as a curiosity. Solo singers have been hastily brought together to 'run through' it. The contraltos have recognized at once that the parts do not suit their voices; the tenor, employed only in the duet 'In vain the amorous flute', has thought the task beneath him. All of them have observed that through long passages the instruments hold chords while they are expected to execute what they regard as singularly angular and inconvenient flourishes. They have gratefully accepted this as a licence to sing out of time and have been content to wobble through somehow. They cannot be blamed for their ignorance of Purcell's style which practically all musicians, and probably, therefore, the conductor who approaches the work as a curiosity, shares with them. I confess that it was not until I undertook to conduct a schoolgirls' performance of *Dido and Aeneas* that I realized the strict-time principle of Purcell's declamation. After that I began to explore his other work in the light of the experience, and understood how the Ode unites this characteristic of his theatrical vocal style with the purely musical qualities which he had gleaned from the *cantilena* of the Italian sonatas.

If a party of singers, solo as well as choral, could be got together to study the 'Ode for St. Cecilia's Day' from the beginning in the way that parties[1] are now studying the 'Operas', the work would soon take its

[1] I allude to productions of *Dido and Aeneas* by Mr. Rutland Boughton's Glastonbury Players, and Mr. Napier Miles's Bristol Opera company, Professor Dent's Cambridge production of *The Fairy Queen* (1911), and that of Mr. Dennis Arundell in London (1927). Since writing the above *King Arthur* has been given on the stage at Cambridge under Dr. C. B. Rootham. Various performances of the 'Operas' without the stage have been given, and the Stirling Choral Society who sang for me at these lectures were then rehearsing *Dido* for a performance of this kind. Professor Dent's influence has also brought *Dido* on to the German stage.

proper place as a great classic of the English concert platform.

When Sir Hugh Allen was resident at Oxford his enthusiasm for Bach led him to gather round him a group of musicians who, meeting privately in his rooms, sang through the whole of the *Bach-Gesellschaft* edition of the cantatas two or three times, devoting a week or so of vacation to the business, and beginning at each meeting where they had broken off at the end of the last.

We have a Purcell Society's Edition (still alas, incomplete) from which at any rate the majority of the anthems, Welcome odes, St. Cecilia odes, and operas might similarly be sung. So far as I am aware no one has ever attempted such a thing, no doubt for the reason which I suggested at the beginning of this lecture, namely, that the musicians capable of organizing a scheme of practical study have conceived a disgust of Purcell in their early youth through their cathedral experience, and have not wished to look farther. The men who have done most to revive Purcell have been scholars not brought up in cathedrals, men like Hubert Parry, who I shall show later was a composer of like spirit with him, Barclay Squire and Fuller Maitland, who saw what his music meant but were not in a position to prove it to others by practice, and Edward Dent, who is even now persuading Englishmen and continentals alike to take the operas seriously. Only one cathedral organist took any conspicuous share in the Purcell revival and that was Frederick Bridge, who in 1895 organized and conducted the bicentenary celebration of his death in Westminster Abbey. But Bridge was an exception in everything. He had the spirit of Samuel Pepys; he explored a little, though not deeply, into things which pleased him, and Purcell pleased him mightily.

CHAPTER VII
HANDEL IN LONDON

IT is safe to say that the name of Handel at once makes every member of a British audience feel at home, whereas the names of several members of that line of British-born composers through whom I have traced the progress of our native song in former chapters have made many of my readers feel anything but at home. With Merbecke, Dowland, and Locke, if not with Purcell, some of you have felt yourselves to be wandering in a foreign land, forming acquaintances with men whose strangeness of language and of manners has limited the sympathy of your approach to them.

With Handel you know where you are. He is more than a name, for his name not only recalls to you a number of different works by him that you know, but a certain kind of music which you would recognize anywhere. If I sit down to the piano and play in this way—

you say at once 'That's Handel', though as a matter of fact it is only a phrase which came into my head on the spur of the moment, and, so far as I know, is not found among his collected works. The name of Handel suggests to our minds at once a broad outline

Voice and Verse

of melody, spaced out in clearly defined periods with well-balanced modulations concluded with conventional perfect cadences.

It may suggest much else, but this much will certainly form part of our conception of the Handelian style. The cadences, though their actual harmonic progression may be the same as those of Purcell or of Bach, strike our ears in Handel as a turn of speech belonging to himself, because he drops into the same melodic formula over and over again at the cadential point, irrespective of what his melody may have been saying before that point was reached. They more than anything else contribute to that comfortable assurance of knowing just where we are with his music. Whatever may be the character of the individual piece, we are quite certain that we shall be given the plain facts of the musical structure without disguise. Purcell will go on surprising us however well we know him; surprising us in both ways, by subtle strokes of genius which give us a sudden sense of discovery, and by curious lapses into weakness or experimentalism. Handel no longer surprises us; he satisfies us by fulfilling expectation.

His whole life and personality presents the most direct contrast to Purcell's, though both spent the greater part of their lives in London grappling with that baffling and still unsolved problem of the Londoner's music. What does the Londoner want from music and why does he so often form a taste only to drop it as soon as a new fashion is brought to him from the Continent? Why does he spoil the artist with adulation in one season and let him pass through the bankruptcy court in the next? These are questions to

Handel in London

which the providers of London's music in opera and concerts are still trying to find the answer. Handel, who was twice made a bankrupt, and Purcell, who successfully opposed the French fashion only to die poor at an early age, faced them, the one by choice, the other by force of circumstances.

Handel was under no obligation to cater for the London public. He was a cosmopolitan if ever there was one. He deserted a post which was probably as lucrative and certainly as secure as Purcell's in order to try his fortune in England. When he came he had already travelled through Central Europe from Hamburg to Naples; he had achieved a reputation in Italy, the very home of his art, which opened to him all the doors in Europe. Having come to this country he need not have stayed. He held no official post, and it is clear from his conduct at Hanover that even if he had held such a post it would not have held him. From childhood he had been of an adventurous spirit, and music-making in London was the most exciting adventure he could find. That was why he stuck to it.

Purcell and Bach were both predestined musicians. They were baptized into music in infancy. Handel chose music against the family tradition and in face of some parental opposition. In Halle, the small country town of Saxony where he was born (1685), and in which his father was a respected citizen, he got from Zachow, the organist, the best and most thorough grounding in that tradition of Lutheran church music, the organ, the chorale, the strict style of choral counterpoint and fugue, which was the natural inheritance of Bach, born the same year at Eisenach. Bach, we know, took long journeys on foot in order to absorb its teaching more thoroughly. Handel took one decisive journey to Hamburg in order to escape from it. There must be something more in the world of music than that system of well-planned rules by which a chorale could be clothed with figuration and a fugue be built up with answer and counter-subject, stretto, and pedal-point. The secret of that something more was at Hamburg, where alone in Germany at the time something like a permanent opera-house existed; Handel went to find it. He made a way for himself in the strange surroundings of Reinhard Keiser's hybrid opera-house in the three or more years which he spent there. Beginning with a minor post as a string-player he advanced to the position of harpsichordist (virtually the conductor's desk), made friends and fought enemies.[1] There he produced operas of his own, and having made his mark he found the provincial circle of Hamburg too small for his ambitions. He got away to Italy ostensibly to study, to drink in music at its fountain-head; actually to conquer it, to beat the Italians on their own ground. From Florence, where he secured the patronage of the powerful Medici family, he proceeded to Rome, where at the Accademia of Cardinal Ottoboni he came in contact with all the brightest minds of the age in music, poetry, and literature. There is a story of how Handel puzzled Corelli, the great violinist, with music for his instrument which was strange to him. In Rome Handel wrote his first oratorio to an allegorical Italian text, *Il trionfo del Tempo e Vero* (the triumph of Time and Truth). His brilliant passage through Italy culminated in the triumph of his opera *Agrippina* at Venice (that city of artists where Monteverdi had established the first home of the opera), when an enthusiastic populace carried him through the streets with cries of 'Il caro Sassone'. He had caught the Italian tone of voice in his melody, the suave unruffled progress which allows the voice to expand itself on the open vowels of the Italian language, the tone which had passed from voice to violin in the sonatas of Corelli, and which years before had appealed to Purcell in his isolation as a mystery without an explanation.

[1] Literally, since his refusal to yield his place at the harpsichord to Johann Mattheson landed him in a duel.

Handel in London

Handel went back to Germany to take up his duties at the small Hanoverian court, a backwater where opera was unknown and music meant only an accompaniment to official piety in the private chapel, and the enlivenment of dreary entertainments outside it. No wonder he chafed against it; any artist would. Bach would have stayed there, writing periodic appeals to other Princelings who might give him better employment. Handel appealed to nobody; he just bided his time and left it, asking official leave the first time, taking 'French leave' the second.

He had his eye on England. He had met Englishmen travelling in Italy. They had said, 'You ought to come to England; you have no idea what a musical public we have,' as Englishmen always do to the foreign musician. They were obviously rich and obviously ignorant. He regarded England, which meant London, as virgin soil, ready to yield to his tillage. So he came. He was only twenty-five years old when he landed at the end of 1710. His leave was short and he intended only a preliminary reconnaissance. He found in London a city very different from that in which Purcell had died fifteen years before, but a very similar society. The face of the town had been further altered by destructive fires and new buildings. The old palace of Whitehall, burnt down in 1698, had been succeeded by St. James's Palace. The Duke of Marlborough had had his seat, Marlborough House, placed cheek by jowl with Queen Anne's palace. The building by Sir Christopher Wren was just completed. The third Earl of Burlington, with whom Handel made friends and with whom he stayed on his second visit, lived at Burlington House in Piccadilly (now the Royal Academy of Arts). Thus fashion was again carrying the town farther west.

During Handel's long life in London the districts of Soho and Bloomsbury sprang up. In the centre of the latter the famous Foundling Hospital, in which

Handel took so practical and beneficent an interest, was placed by its founder, Coram, in 1742. Mayfair became a favourite residential neighbourhood. Handel bought a house in Brook Street when he had determined to settle in London, and he lived in it from 1721 until his death.

At the time of his arrival the ancient city had been rehabilitated after the Great Fire, its churches and public buildings had been laid out on the designs of Wren with St. Paul's Cathedral as centrepiece.

Along with the process of church-building had gone that of organ-building, an art led largely by Purcell's friend Bernhard Schmitt, who had been naturalized and was familiarly known as 'Father Smith', a nickname which attested his pre-eminence in his art. Two of Smith's organs in London are specially famous, that which he placed in the Temple Church, and on which Purcell played, and that which he built for St. Paul's Cathedral. Wren, who was not musical, grudged the space in the cathedral required by what he called 'the damned box of whistles'. However, he had to allow it place in a conspicuous position right in the centre of the chancel arch, and there it was, cased in the fine carving of Grinling Gibbons, ready for Handel's performance.

Handel's London, then, was much nearer to the London of to-day than to Purcell's London. Most of its familiar landmarks, from St. Paul's to Marlborough House were there, looking clean and new, no doubt, but the same that we know.

In one further important particular the face of the town had changed. Dorset Garden had given way to the Queen's Theatre, built by Vanbrugh in the Haymarket in 1706, and there society had already been given a taste of the Italian opera which had whetted an appetite for more entertainment of that exotic and therefore sensational kind. The Queen's Theatre was to be the scene of Handel's first triumphs. Later, when it was renamed the King's Theatre, he occupied it and

Handel in London

provided its entertainments through a long series of years with varying success until in 1734 he transferred himself and his company to the newly opened Covent Garden Theatre.

Londoners therefore can trace in their opera-houses a long line of history which begins with Handel. The site, though not the building of the original Queen's Theatre, revived its association with foreign Opera in the nineteenth century, when Her Majesty's Theatre became the home of a galaxy of brilliant singers. The Royal Opera Arcade hard by it still exists, and Sir Herbert Tree built his theatre of the same name on the same site, and in it Sir Thomas Beecham's earlier operatic seasons were given. The succession of operatic ventures at Covent Garden has been even more continuous up to the present day.

In the interval between the death of Purcell and the arrival of Handel there had been sporadic efforts to carry on the production of that pseudo-opera which had been at once Purcell's opportunity and his despair, and which he had dignified with his music in such works as *The Fairy Queen* and *King Arthur*. His brother, Daniel Purcell, had contributed to the genre; so had John Eccles, whose setting of *Semele* was never performed, though the book subsequently became famous through Handel's music to it. Thomas Clayton had produced Addison's *Rosamund* as an opera; its failure presumably rankled and partially accounted for the tone of bitter satire in which Addison wrote of Handel's opera in *The Spectator* when it took the town by storm. Sir Richard Steele was producing drama at Drury Lane, and as Steele was Addison's friend the success of foreign competition in the rival house could hardly be welcome to Addison, even had there not been the direct incentive of personal pique to urge him to the attack.[1]

Handel entered an enlarged London with an enlarged society which was no longer the small coterie of

[1] See Burney's *History of Music*, vol. iv, chap. 6.

courtiers grouped around the person of the monarch and taking its tone from him, as had been the case in the second Stuart era. It was a society in which different views could be more freely expressed in literature and criticism, and even the journalist was beginning to feel his power. This state of things was to expand much farther during the period of Handel's own life. The factions and feuds of society caused him many embarrassments and bitter disappointments; they also enabled him to create in time a party for himself, a party which dictated British musical taste for a century after his death.

For the moment, however, apart from Addison and his friends, Handel was greeted with the same enthusiasm which had been given to the later works of Purcell. He was going to show the town what real Italian opera was like. He wrote a new work, *Rinaldo*, in hot haste, incorporating some of the songs from previous efforts of the kind, assembled the best company of singers available, and secured its production at the Queen's Theatre on 24 February 1711, with the additional attraction of the most brilliant stage spectacle for the scene of Armida's garden that the resources of the theatre could command. The effect was electric. Society was completely carried off its feet and Handel was the sensation of the season. He had not much time for more; he had to leave London early in June and return to his duties at Hanover. But he left with the determination to return as soon as possible, and this he actually did in the autumn of the following year (1712).

It is no part of my concern here to trace out Handel's operatic career in London. The point I want to make decisively is that Handel came to this country with one primary purpose in view, to supply the wealthy classes of a prosperous city with the fashionable entertainment called the Italian opera. He intended only to give a taste of his genius and then decamp with the fruits of his labours as other foreign artists had done before and

Handel in London

have done more frequently since. The unprecedented success of his first visit made a second irresistible. He came back and stayed. The place grew on him and he grew into it. Though he never could master the subtleties of the English language (his gutteral and ungrammatical speech was a popular jest of the time) he became an Englishman not only by virtue of his nationalization papers, which he obtained subsequently, but very largely in thought and feeling, tastes and sympathies.

For thirty years he pursued stubbornly his curious aim of planting Italian opera in British soil, and was not deflected by the fact that one planting after another withered despite the most assiduous husbandry on his part. His misdirected energy was displayed in four periods. The first was one of ill-organized effort at the Queen's Theatre, in the course of which a certain manager, MacSwiney by name, disappeared, taking the cash-box with him. His place was taken by Heidegger, known as the 'Swiss Count', an eccentric but able individual, whose reputation as the ugliest man in London was in itself a valuable advertisement to any venture with which he associated himself. Handel worked with Heidegger successfully and repeatedly throughout his career. After a few years in which Handel was otherwise occupied, how it will presently appear, he returned to the charge as chief composer to what was almost a state-aided opera, an institution started with a large capital and called the Royal Academy of Music. It lasted eight years (1720–8), was torn to pieces by the rival factions who first pitted Handel and Bononcini against one another, and then, when the latter was driven from the field, indulged in equally futile contests about the rival merits of the female singers, Cuzzoni and Faustina. Finally it was done to death by Gay's brilliant jibe, *The Beggar's Opera*, which not only satirized the absurdities of the Italian opera but created a new sensation of simplicity. Society deserted the Royal Academy of Music at the

King's Theatre and flocked to Lincoln's Inn Fields to revel in the rascally humours and ungarnished English ballads which Gay brought together to tickle their palates.

All this might have taught Handel the impossibility of his task, but not a bit of it. He instantly went into management himself and started a third operatic venture on his own responsibility at the King's Theatre. The answer of his opponents to this move was a rival house called 'The Opera of the Nobility', which succeeded in capturing his theatre when his lease ran out a few years later. It was then that he made a fresh start at Covent Garden, but this, too, ended in bankruptcy and the complete breakdown of his health. After this, even, he continued to write operas, but chiefly at the request of Heidegger. Handel himself had discovered another type of entertainment for the town, the oratorio, in which he was destined to make good as no other man has before or since.

Behind all these operatic failures there lurked a lesson which may seem obvious enough to us, but which Handel was extremely loath to learn, and which many people have still not learnt. Foreign opera involves deception. Handel, a German composing Italian opera for English audiences, was pretending; the English audiences which alternately crowded and emptied the opera-house were also pretending. Handel virtually said to his audience, Never mind what it is all about, just enjoy these agreeable sounds brought agreeably to your ears by people whose whole lives have been devoted to acquiring the power of making agreeable sounds. The audience in return said: Let's pretend we do understand; since the drama is meaningless and the language unintelligible, let us show our acumen by judging between one composer and another or between one singer and another. The lesson which Handel refused to learn, and his refusal cost him dear, was that if you present works of art to people who have not the means to bring their understanding to bear on essential qualities, they will inevitably glance aside to what is not essential and concern themselves with the trimmings which they can understand. The whole case against foreign opera, whether that of Handel or any one else, has been stated concisely by the first Cramb lecturer in the remark that 'Art reaches our feelings always *through* the understanding. It is not, like logic and grammar, an appeal *to* the understanding, but aims at a goal whose only approach is *through* the understanding.'[1] Handel's operatic audience could not understand the Italian language; perhaps, for all his early experience he could only half understand it, as he only half understood the English language. He busied himself in trying to make up to himself and to them for the lack of understanding, with the result that the English people, or at any rate London people, imbibed a false conception of what opera is which they have never outgrown and which it is doubtful whether they ever can outgrow.

Stubbornly as Handel resisted this lesson he began to learn one or two others almost as soon as he definitely settled himself down to life in England. The country was not quite the virgin soil for his music which he had supposed it to be when he planned his first meteoric visit to it. It possessed some music of its own, some traditions and some preconceived notions of style which might be worth his attention. Handel was a great man, and in nothing showed himself so great as in the fact that he was never above learning. As he had learnt from Hamburg, from Florence and Rome, so he began to learn from England.

The new organ soon attracted him to St. Paul's Cathedral, and he played on it after service till the vergers complained that they could not get the congregation out. In the cathedral service he found music of a kind which was new to him, perhaps rather crabbed, but still something distinct from either the Lutheran

[1] *The Scope of Music*, p. 46.

habits of his youth or the great Roman tradition he had met with in Italy. Before the death of Queen Anne he had the opportunity of composing two works which showed his contact with English habits of mind both in and out of church, and especially a bowing acquaintance with the scores of Purcell. He was asked for a Te Deum and Jubilate to celebrate the Peace of Utrecht and an ode to celebrate the Queen's birthday (6 Feb. 1713). In both he wanted to please, to do something in accordance with a recognized taste in such things, and Purcell gave him his cue alike in the Cecilian Te Deum and Jubilate and the several welcome odes. In both Handel's scores one sees at once the effort to reproduce and extend Purcell's style of vocal ornamentation, particularly in the liberal use of that dotted note figure of which Purcell was undoubtedly too fond. The Utrecht Te Deum and Jubilate in D replaced Purcell's work in the same key at the annual Festival of the Sons of the Clergy in St. Paul's (1713). It was much admired. Streatfeild[1] says that 'Handel's mighty strength of wing had already left Purcell far behind'. No doubt he is right from the purely musical point of view. I have already tried to show how Purcell had striven blindly to acquire that strength of wing from the Italian style which Italy herself had bestowed on Handel. But Handel here and in all his English works also lagged far behind in sensitiveness towards language, which was the mainspring of Purcell's native art. In Handel's vocal work the Purcellian ornaments seem stuck on with an eye to general effectiveness rather than to emphasize some idea implied by the words.

The poem given him for the ode was of the same kind of sycophantic doggerel as that on which Purcell had been made to spend himself in the welcome odes to William and Mary. Each stanza had the refrain

> The day that gave great Anna birth,
> Who fix'd a lasting peace on earth.

[1] *Handel*, p. 262.

Handel in London

For its performance Handel had the Purcellian orchestra (trumpets, oboes, strings), the best English singers available, Mrs. Robinson and Mrs. Barbie, male altos called Elford (Handel wrote his name 'Eilfurt') and Hughes, with other 'Gentlemen of the Chapel Royal', and its full choir for the choral parts. Handel led off the first stanza with a male alto solo, perhaps laughing in his sleeve a little as he wrote it:

He expended much choral ingenuity on the several returns of the refrain, carried instrumental figures on from the solo numbers into the choruses, made a vigorous point with a duet for alto and bass on a 'ground bass' (the bass itself a much more emphatic figure than those which Purcell loved to use as backgrounds), introduced a 'Siciliano' rhythm in a duet for the two women, and ended with a large scale movement for all the voices and instruments. The word went forth that the new-comer had beaten the Englishman on his own ground and posterity has accepted that decision of the umpires as final. Such composers as there were (they were not considerable) set themselves to write Handelian music for the future. One of them, Dr. Boyce,[1] tried to rescue Purcell's Te Deum from oblivion by fattening it out with instrumental *ritornelli*

---

[1] See Bridge's edition of Purcell's Te Deum (Novello), which shows what Boyce had done to it.

and other additions in the big Handelian manner. Thus, though Handel did not kill English music, he caused it to be stuffed.

Handel evidently respected Purcell as far as he could understand him, but he had no more real understanding of him than his own English audiences had of his Italian opera. He could see only the externals. He never 'borrowed' Purcell's music, as he borrowed that of continental contemporaries and predecessors. Perhaps his restraint in this matter means that he gave his English audiences credit, which they certainly did not deserve, for knowledge of their native master. A fine chorus, on a chromatic ground bass ('How long, O Lord'), in Handel's oratorio *Susanna* has been pointed to as copied from Dido's lament. It certainly bears a strong likeness, though the bass itself is closer to Bach's Crucifixus in the B minor Mass than to Purcell's. The harmonic development is like an extension of Purcell's instrumental peroration. They deserve comparison, but they are by no means identical.

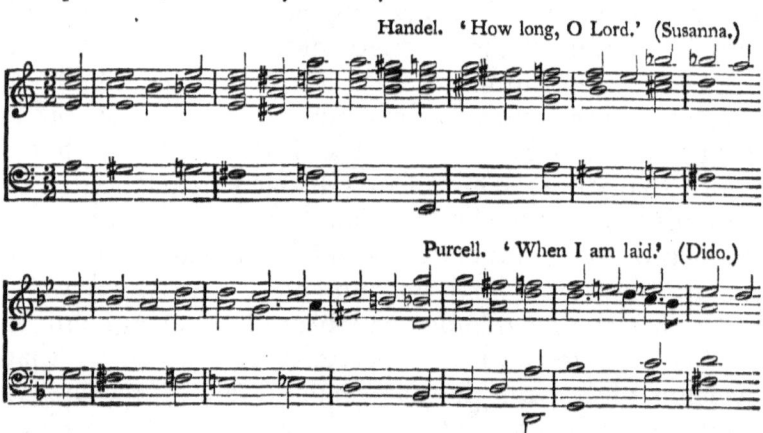

An interesting instance of Handel taking a wrinkle from Purcell's style, but totally misconceiving its purpose, is the chorus 'Queen of Summer' in another oratorio, *Theodora*. Often, when writing in a triple measure, Purcell would throw some of the accents on

Handel in London

to the second beat of the bar with the manifest purpose of neutralizing the emphasis on the first of the bar for the sake of the words. It gave him two accents instead of one in a bar of ¾ time. It destroyed the 'thud' of such a time and enabled him to stress important syllables which could not be brought on to the initial accent of the bar. The following are instances in poetry and prose from secular and sacred song respectively:

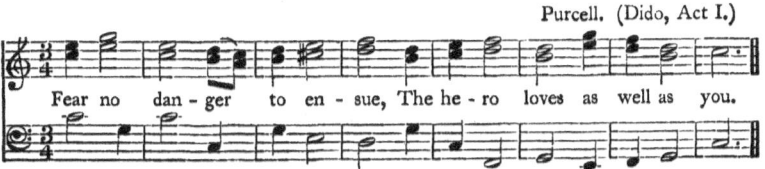
Purcell. (Dido, Act I.)
Fear no dan - ger to en - sue, The he - ro loves as well as you.

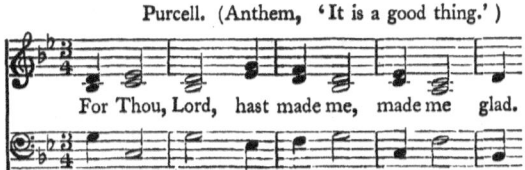
Purcell. (Anthem, 'It is a good thing.')
For Thou, Lord, hast made me, made me glad.

The *naïveté* of this evidently took Handel's fancy; he thought it very pretty. So when he wanted something naïve and pretty, something suggestive of summer time and love, he started off light-heartedly with

Handel. (Theodora, Act II.)
Queen of Sum - mer, Queen of Love.

and forced through his chorus according to sample, regardless of verbal chaos and of the enormities involved in such a line as

Grant *a* long and hap*py* reign.

English critics who ought to know better have ever since pointed with admiration to the Purcellian flavour of this ludicrous caricature.

The finer contacts of song with the English language always remained quite outside Handel's consciousness. But though he could never feel the language, he was too instinctive an artist to remain unaffected by other contacts with the land of his adoption. Those years between his first and his second operatic periods which were largely spent in the country as chief musician to the Duke of Chandos who had built himself a palace at Canons near Edgware, probably did more to bring Handel into touch with the English character than all his experience of London life could do. It must be remembered that after the death of Queen Anne a German king sat on the English throne (Handel's neglected master of Hanover), who brought German manners and customs to court just as Charles II had brought the French when Purcell was a boy.

Once George I had got over his pique at Handel's misdemeanour, the Germanizing influence was in his favour socially, but it did not help him to understand the English character which remained unaffected by court fashions. A country life could help him. It was a piece of good fortune for Handel that James Brydges, the war profiteer, thought to add to his newly-created ducal splendours by securing the man of the hour as his chief musician, and carried Handel out of London to Canons. The duke's chapel was to rival the royal chapel; singers were engaged and Handel wrote for them that remarkable series of works still known as the Chandos Anthems. They show how his memory harked back to the church music of his Lutheran days, how he mixed with it the aria types of the Italian solo cantatas and operas and seasoned the mixture with the style of the Anglican anthem as Purcell had developed it. They are more cantatas than anthems, however, too large to take a place as part of the ritual of a Church Office. What must have been more important to him than the composition of such works was the opportunity the post gave him of mixing with the singers, who, though they were men of much smaller experience than himself, had grown up in the English traditions of song, had their own tastes, and were able to give him samples of the national taste in secular and church music.

Moreover, at Canons and its neighbourhood he must have come across the simple English people, the farmers and villagers who knew nothing of his art and who would regard him, as such people always regard the foreigner, as some one a little unfortunate and probably half-witted, to whom they ought to be kind. The story of Handel sheltering in the blacksmith's forge at Edgware and writing 'The Harmonious Blacksmith' in consequence, has long since been proved a forgery in the most literal sense, but though we know next to nothing of his daily life at Canons we do know that he was a man who never shut himself up from his fellows or played the great artist in private life, and that he was a man of sturdy physique and unbounded energy. It is scarcely fanciful to suppose that he began to be an Englishman from the time that he got into the English country.

Two entertainments he made for the ducal court at Canons outside the chapel music were the masque of *Esther* (founded on an English version of Racine) and that of *Acis and Galatea*. As the first dramatic works with English texts they are of supreme importance in the story of Handel's progress in English ways. A tablet fixed to the organ in the parish church of Canons (which was not the ducal chapel) gives the interesting information that Handel composed his 'Divine Oratorio' on this organ. Quite apart from the fact that Handel never composed, except when he improvised, on or at an instrument at all (only the most incompetent amateurs ever do that) he had no thought of composing a 'Divine Oratorio' at this time. Though *Esther* was founded on a play with a Biblical subject it was in its first form a secular dramatic entertainment like *Acis and Galatea,* an attempt to revive and improve on the

English masques of earlier days which had added to the festivities of many a country house party. Whatever his own predilections might be (and all the time his heart was set on Italian opera) he was ready to try anything and everything in which his music might give pleasure. If the English had artistic traditions which they valued he was quite prepared to enter into them. He only wanted to know what they were.

While he was turning out anthems and masques in the country, London Society determined that it must have some more Italian opera and called Handel back to direct the Royal Academy of Music. He came, nothing loath. After all, that was to him the grand style; he threw himself with renewed energy into supplying what was wanted, and forgot all about *Esther* for a dozen years or so. When it was recalled to his mind it gave him the new idea he was seeking for. That idea was the English oratorio.

CHAPTER VIII
THE ORATORIO

A GLANCE at any reliable portrait of Handel shows you that he was at once a very practical and a very obstinate man. His obstinacy would not allow him to give way before an obstacle, but his practicality would enable him to find a way round it when direct advance had become impossible. That was what happened when Frederick, Prince of Wales, gave his support to the 'Opera of the Nobility', not so much from any desire to advance the art, as in the hope of annoying his royal father, King George II, who gave his patronage to Handel's venture. It was clear from the first that London could not support two operas; it was very doubtful whether it would maintain one for long.

The 'Opera of the Nobility' determined Handel's resolve to pursue further an idea which had come to him in the year before his rival started operations. He had by this time attained a position as an accepted factor in London life. This informal recognition was more important to him than his naturalization papers or the appointment of 'Composer to the Chapel Royal' which had brought him the commission to write the anthems for the coronation of George II. It was in 1732 that the Chapel Royal boys prepared a birthday compliment for him in a private performance of *Esther*, which had been put on the shelf since his Canons days. Its success before a limited audience was so distinct that an enterprising manager saw money in it, and actually announced a piratical performance. That decided Handel. He announced a performance of *Esther* to be given in the King's Theatre 'by His Majesty's Command'.

The advertisement of this performance bears an interesting footnote:

N.B. There will be no acting on the stage, but the house will be fitted up in a decent manner for the audience. The Musick [*i.e.* the performers] will be disposed after the manner of the Coronation Service.

It was necessary to explain the new arrangement, because *Esther* had originally been not a 'Divine Oratorio' but a dramatic piece, and the coronation service, in which choir and orchestra were ranged in tiers, as they are in any modern oratorio performance, was the only function offering a precedent which all would recognize for this novel entertainment. The description is significant as an indication of how the idea of oratorio emerged from that of the anthem enlarged by Handel to the dimensions of a choral cantata. Handel was a great impresario. When the 'Opera of the Nobility' opened its doors he realized the value of a 'feature' which his rivals could not copy. Nicolò Porpora, the composer on whom that institution principally depended, might turn out arias as polished as his own, if less inspired. Certainly Porpora, who was one of the great singing teachers for the Italian stage, could supply work which would serve even better than Handel's to show off the singer's powers. The rival opera filched his best singers from him and later on, as has been already said, it got possession of the theatre which he had occupied for so long. Everything seemed to be turning against him, but his own genius both as impresario and composer saved him ultimately.

He followed up the concert versions of *Esther* and *Acis* with *Deborah*, the first of his Biblical oratorios originally intended for that kind of performance, and one in which he lavished all his great resources on powerful choruses. This showed his good sense. He was in something of a difficulty about singers, for the language made it impossible to employ his Italian company in work of this kind. In turning to oratorio he had to put his faith in English singers, and his experience of London choirs, the Chapel Royal, St. Paul's, Westminster Abbey and the Festival of the Sons of the Clergy, told him that their strength lay in their team work, and that therefore the chorus, not the soloists, must be the protagonists in his new form of musical drama.

The Oratorio

Long before, Matthew Locke, in that plea for an English opera to which reference has been made (see Chapter IV), had said that he despaired of ever finding voices in England equal to those of Italy. Handel, with a far wider practical experience of both nations than Locke had, appreciated that capacity for blending in ensemble which makes our English choirs to-day the finest in the world. He had also had time to discern that quality of the English temperament, diametrically opposed to the Latin, which rejoices and excels in corporate effort; which makes the schoolboys play games 'for the school', turns eight indifferent oars into a boat capable of making bumps and fills the church steeples with peals rather than with carillons.

Deborah ought not to be forgotten as it is, for not only is it magnificent music but it attests Handel's faith in the English choral capacity, and further it shows Handel's perception of the fact that oratorio could not be justified merely as opera with 'no acting on the stage', but must represent a point of view towards its subject-matter distinct from that of opera.

The latter had become the accepted vehicle for the *stile rappresentativo*. However much the opera might have been diverted from its original purpose by the formal enlargement of the aria, direct representation of characters and events was its basis; its persons spoke always in *oratio recta*. In the oratorio, with the musicians in plain clothes and 'disposed after the manner of the Coronation Service', *oratio obliqua* was more appropriate. The assumption of direct representation involves an inherent absurdity quite as provocative of laughter as those absurdities of which English people are always so excessively conscious in the opera.

To take a familiar example from Mendelssohn's *Elijah*, there would be nothing absurd on the stage in the meeting of a king and a demagogue, and the one taunting the other with having upset the peace of his kingdom. It is merely a conversational incident necessary to the progress of the drama. But when Ahab (tenor) and Elijah (bass) stand up one on each side of the conductor and snarl at one another like two dogs kennelled just out of one another's reach, 'Art thou he that troubleth Israel?' . . . 'I never troubled Israel's peace. It is thou, Ahab' &c., the effect is bound to be comical. The sense of unfitness is irresistible.

The only escape from such moments of bathos is to treat the oratorio as an epic rather than as a narrative, to make it rather the celebration of great deeds, religious and heroic, than the representation of the characters employed in them. That was why Handel chose the story of Deborah, summed up in the epic hymn with which the prophetess celebrated her triumph over the enemies of the Lord (Judges v).

But there is another side from which Handel's innovation must be viewed. Later commentators have repeatedly dwelt on the edifying nature of the Biblical histories on which he built his oratorios, in contrast with the unedifying themes of sexual passion and intrigue which have formed the basis of opera in all ages, and not least in Handel's own. A legend has been built up of Handel as a great moralist, who harnessed his art to the service of religion, and my suggestion that he stumbled on it in the course of his search for a new form of entertainment may seem unworthy, if not actually profane, to those who have been brought up on that legend. If this more prosaic view is true, why, it may reasonably be asked, did he search his Bible through and through for inspiring themes, and what about that oft-related story of his reproof to the gentleman who after the production of *Messiah* congratulated him on the fine entertainment he had given the town. 'My Lord,' Handel is reported to have said, 'I should be sorry if I only entertained them; I wished to make them better.'

The story may be true, for Handel certainly did wish to make his English audiences better; no one ever laboured more assiduously to that end. A man of his

The Oratorio

artistic perception must have despised the frivolity, the backbiting and the chit-chat of the society for which he had undertaken to cater. But it does not follow that the words, if he used them, were uttered with the pietistic unction which the subsequent report gave to them. There were many sides to Handel's character. He might say a thing like that with becoming earnestness, meaning by it more than his hearers could fathom, especially just after one of the great inspirations of his life. Again, when he was about to produce *Theodora* he could cynically predict its failure on the grounds that the Jews would not like it because it was Christian and the ladies would not like it because it was virtuous. He required all his sense of humour to carry him through his task.

It was his realization of the epic character of oratorio which sent him to the Bible for his subjects. He laid no embargo on secular themes, but on the whole they served him less well than 'sacred' ones. He found a good libretto in Dryden's *Alexander's Feast* and a little later in the same poet's *Ode on St. Cecilia's Day*. He allowed Charles Jennens to make an extraordinary hotch-potch for his music from Milton's 'L'Allegro' and 'Il Penseroso', picked up the old English opera libretto of *Semele* which Eccles had set years ago and used it for an oratorio. In short, he spread his net as wide as possible, and was willing to try anything and everything which would submit to his particular artistic medium. With some of these, notably with *Semele* and *Susanna*, he turned again towards the unstaged opera type with which he had begun. The story of Susanna and the Elders may have an edifying moral (did Handel know how popular it had been as a lyric theme for the madrigalists?) but it is certainly far from being 'sacred', and Handel only just kept it in touch with religious conventions of the day by the insertion of a few choruses such as the 'How long, O Lord', quoted in the last chapter (see p. 116).

The Bible stories served Handel's purpose best because an epic can only appeal by celebrating that which is known. Though the Christian religion had sunk to a low ebb under the Erastian Church of the Hanoverian kings, the English people in the first half of the eighteenth century did know their Bible history as they knew scarcely any other literature. Not only did they know it, but they identified it with themselves. They were the Chosen People, at any rate in their own eyes. The Continent was given over to papistry and the black arts. (Did not these very Italians who came to entertain them at the opera produce their voices by unnatural means too horrid to be described?)

> The nations not so blest as thee
> Must in their turn to tyrants fall,
> But thou shalt flourish great and free,
> The dread and envy of them all.

'Rule, Britannia' secured immortality from the fine tune with which Thomas Arne endowed it; it attained immediate popularity because the tone and temper of the words were those of the time; the verses said what Englishmen really thought and felt about the destiny of their country.

An epic has been defined[1] as 'a poem embodying a nation's conception of its past history', and the definition requires only a little expansion to include Handel's Biblical oratorios. For 'nation' read 'people' and by people mean the people of the Lord, whether ancient Jews or eighteenth-century Britons, and the epic appeal of Handel to his own generation is explained. In them patriotic heroism was exalted; the triumph of the Lord's people meant the triumph of righteousness; righteousness meant the supremacy of British interests and the security of the Protestant Succession. In *Judas Maccabaeus*, written to celebrate the victory at Culloden, the whole process of associated thought is revealed.

Handel might occasionally be a little cynical about it,

[1] The *Oxford English Dictionary*.

but he belonged to his time, and his capacity to become the spokesman for this typically British ideal shows how completely he had identified himself with his adopted country since those early days when he sat down to make a perfunctory copy of the Purcellian odes for Queen Anne's birthday.

From the time of the collapse of both opera-houses, his own and his rival's (1738), Handel devoted the best of his creative energies to the composition of oratorios. The year 1739 was a very productive one. It began with *Saul*. *Israel in Egypt*, planned as a sort of trilogy, the parts of which were, like those of Wagner's *Ring*, thought out and partially composed in reverse order, followed in April. The autumn saw his setting of Dryden's *Ode on St. Cecilia's Day*, which affords the most direct link between the methods of Handel and of Purcell.

In *Deborah* he had plunged too boldly into the grand style of the choral epic for the taste of his audience. He probably realized this, and *Saul* is a tactful blend of the dramatic with the epic. The first scene framed by the chorus, 'How excellent is Thy name', alludes to, rather than relates, the story of David and Goliath. The 'Infant raised at Thy command' is pictured in a high soprano solo and contrasted with the giant Goliath, the heavy tread of whose theme reminds the modern hearer of Fasolt and Fafner. But no sooner is the Philistine fallen and the rout celebrated with its appropriate 'Hallelujah', than David and Saul, Abner, Jonathan, and the two daughters of Saul (Merab and Michal), appear in their own persons and converse in frankly operatic recitative. The domestic details of their conversation, particularly the discussion as to which of the sisters is to marry David, is not very good dramatic material, though it might be tolerable on the stage. In oratorio it is quite misplaced. Handel seems to forget his epic opening and goes on in the manner of the opera to introduce a dance and song of maidens with picturesque carillon (*Glockenspiel*) accompaniment, presently joined by the male chorus singing 'David his ten thousands slew', the episode which arouses Saul's jealousy. Saul's song 'A serpent in my bosom warmed' breaks off abruptly in the minor key (having begun in the major) with a rushing downward scale on the strings. This is intended to depict the action of Saul throwing his javelin at David, like the harp *glissando* with which Wagner makes Klingsor throw the spear at Parsifal, but as neither words nor action accompany Handel's scale, the audience has to depend on previous knowledge of the story to realize the significance of the musical point. So the story is continued in a way which, except for the occasional reflective choruses, is entirely that of drama. It includes long conversations between Saul and Jonathan, a love duet for David and Michal, and the powerfully conceived scene between Saul and the Witch of Endor in which the ghost of Samuel is raised to the hollow-sounding background of bassoons.

All this ought to be put on the stage, as indeed some of Handel's more dramatic oratorios have been in recent years. Had it not been for the British prejudice against the acting of Biblical subjects Handel would probably have staged it himself. But all the time he was enacting this unstaged opera he had in prospect the wonderful lament of David for Saul and Jonathan which begins with the famous 'Dead March'. Though unfortunately the libretto of *Saul* is not made out of the words of the Bible but is in doggerel verse, Handel's musical treatment of the lament with solo voices and chorus in combination recovers the essential nobility and pathos of the passage which has for its refrain,

How are the mighty fallen.

The short numbers which succeed one another in a striking sequence of keys[1] are knit together in a symphonic design and culminate in a concerted number

---

[1] Compare Purcell's Elegy on Playford, p. 95.

The Oratorio

(soprano solo with chorus) 'O fatal day', which is one of the most deeply moving things Handel ever wrote. Here drama has given way to epic contemplation. Moreover, Handel's splendid sense of emotional balance leads him to sweep away the elegiac mood in a virile finale chorus 'Gird on thy sword'.

I have dwelt in some detail on *Saul* because it, coming as it does between *Deborah* and *Israel in Egypt*, shows Handel hesitating in a significant fashion between his new-found epic manner and the opera with 'no acting on the stage'. With *Israel*, beginning with the Song of Miriam and then going back to the story of the plagues of Egypt told in a series of descriptive choruses, which stand like roughly drawn cartoons on a large canvas, he once more put the theatre out of his mind. His partial return to the operatic manner in the later Old Testament oratorios, notably in *Samson* (founded on Milton), *Belshazzar*, *Judas Maccabaeus*, and *Jephthah*, shows that he had not completely cleared his mind on the difference of outlook which the two forms require.

Beethoven is said to have professed that he always composed to a picture. Whether or not that is true of Beethoven, it is certainly true of Handel, and his picture was always framed by a proscenium. He had the keenest sense for a striking theatrical situation, and where his subject-matter gave him one he invariably responded to it with directly theatrical music. In *Belshazzar*, for example, one sees him preparing for the denouement of the writing on the wall in the way he elaborates the scene of the king's revels. He assembles the whole company, complete with *corps de ballet*, on the stage and gives Belshazzar a rollicking drinking song, glass in hand, in front of the footlights. When the merriment is at its height, detached staccato notes on the violins begin slowly to trace out the inscrutable legend. The revels are thrown into confusion; the king cries out and faints, exclamations of fear and horror proceed from the courtiers. Verdi himself could not have done the thing more effectively from the stage point of view.

In this way Handel's ineradicable theatricalism, his knowledge of his public (with whom he kept in close touch as a good impresario must), and his ideal perception of what was appropriate to the form of art he had chosen, all mingled as ingredients in his oratorio form. A fastidious taste may easily pick holes in the result, and call his oratorio an illogical hybrid basing its appeal on extraneous sentiment. There is some truth in such objections, but they weigh light in the balance against his positive achievement. Handel found in it the means of stirring to appreciation of, and participation in, great music literally millions of people unborn when he wrote, who would have remained outside and completely unaffected by music but for his hybrid. For at least a hundred years after his death the English-speaking peoples lived on Handel's oratorios, because, using the dramatic and the epic manner alternately, he treated in them the emotions of the Biblical characters they represented as though they were those of the simple people who formed the audiences or sang in the choruses.

I have purposely left *Messiah* out of count so far because it holds a position apart in the affections of the majority which still makes it almost impossible to discuss it frankly without offending susceptibilities which I wish to respect. I would suggest, however, that my analysis of Handel's approach to oratorio really covers the case of *Messiah* equally with the rest. Its history does not suggest that he approached it in any different spirit. Charles Jennens, who put together several librettos for him, had the idea of an oratorio on the redemption of mankind through the Incarnation, Passion, and Resurrection of the Saviour. It was to be an epic of the Christian religion. Fortunately for the work itself and for posterity he had the good sense to realize that for such a theme the words of the Prophets, of the Gospel story, of St. Paul's Epistles, and the Revelation

The Oratorio

of St. John, as given in the English Bible, would be more potent than any versifying of his own. His selection of texts, from 'Comfort ye, my people' to 'Worthy is the Lamb that was slain', was masterly, almost a work of genius in itself, and Jennens seems to have been fully conscious of his own achievement. He is reported to have said that Mr. Handel had made a fine thing of his *Messiah*, though not nearly so fine a thing as he might have done. We are none of us in a position to gainsay such a criticism. Handel, writing with intense rapidity as usual and taking many ideas from his own earlier works, might, no doubt, have considered many details of expression more carefully, as Bach did in treating a similar theme. Handel's instrumentation in *Messiah* is notably deficient as compared, for example, with the score of *Saul*. There are many signs that he took no exceptional trouble in the act of composition. But working in his own way, and guided by that enormous sense of proportion which had already produced *Israel*, he rose to the height of his opportunity, and produced a work which for boldness of design and sustained vigour, though he used only the simplest of musical terms, is unrivalled in the whole range of musical art. Had Handel undertaken the task in a more introspective spirit, more in accordance with that desire to edify which has been attributed to him, he would have been liable to miss just that quality in his music which has sent the message of *Messiah* out into all lands.

Here we encounter that paradox which underlies the whole relation of words and music in the art of song. We have seen the English art growing in the work of a series of composers who consistently sought for a more intimate connexion between language and music. Handel comes with his tremendous power of melody and a cosmopolitan outlook oblivious of all the finer suggestions which the language can offer him, and, taking texts from the purest source of English literature, allies them to music which makes a universal appeal in spite of, one might almost say because of, his obliviousness. No English composer with any sensitiveness to, or respect for, his own language could have set the plain monosyllables of 'For unto us a child is born' to the trite fugue subject ending in an extravagant roulade which Handel chose from one of his Italian duets for the purpose. In itself the thing is a monstrous impertinence, but it takes its place in his architectonic scheme and only a pedant would complain of it. It is justified in the purely musical design, just as Belshazzar's song is justified in the histrionic design, by the outcome from it.

Having traced the process of Handel's spiritual naturalization in England up to the point of his greatest oratorio, and noted also the twin process of what may be called the 'Handelisation' of musical England, it is reasonable to inquire how far his lyrical song was actually affected by English thought and feeling and its expression in the language. One more direct contrast with Purcell may clinch the matter, and his setting of Dryden's *Ode on St. Cecilia's Day* (originally written for 1687 but set by Handel in 1739, the year of *Saul* and *Israel*) affords a good opportunity. In the tenor song with chorus, 'The trumpet's loud clangour excites us to arms', Handel has words identical in feeling and almost in expression with those which the same poet gave to Purcell in ' "Come if you dare," our trumpets sound' in *King Arthur*. Purcell's setting is also a tenor song with chorus, and there are other obvious similarities in the musical treatment. One can scarcely suppose Handel's to have been quite independent of the earlier composer,

Handel.

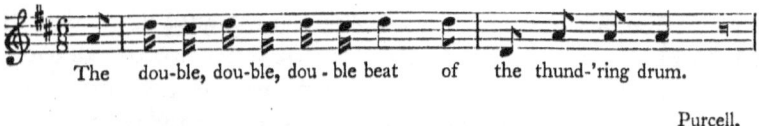

The dou-ble, dou-ble, dou-ble beat of the thund-'ring drum.

Purcell.

The dou-ble, dou-ble, dou-ble beat of the thund - 'ring drum.

The Oratorio

though his 'The thund'ring drum' shows him to be still quite reckless about the verbal accentuation which Purcell guarded instinctively. But it is in the initial idea that they contrast most forcibly. Purcell's has sprung out of the words; Handel's out of the sound of the trumpet, though the two have roughly the same melodic outline.

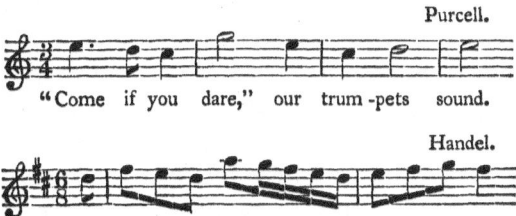

Purcell fulfils completely the conditions which we saw at the outset of our inquiry go to make the perfect union of words and music in song. Handel is seized by their feeling, catches at their general sense, and straightway a tune comes into his head which accords with them. The details then have to be fitted more or less mechanically and not always successfully, while that tune develops on purely musical lines. Purcell's song is strophic, the chorus echoing each half strophe of the solo; Handel's song is worked out in aria form with central modulations and returns to the original key before the chorus enters. When it does so its musical development is still more expansive and achieves a climax of great musical vigour but in which the several verbal phrases are inextricably jumbled together.

Handel was always sensitive to the mood of words, only partially susceptible to their rhythm or lilt, and entirely impervious to their shape. The shape of a song was for him an exclusively musical affair, and his inventive genius was so abundant that he easily persuaded all who came in contact with him that his was the right, indeed the only, point of view possible for the musician.

After him the highest ambition of English song-writers was to discover a good tune which would fit approximately to the chosen words, if possible a tune more or less of the kind which Handel himself might have written punctuated with his typical cadences. As they had little of his sensitiveness to mood and none of his musical fertility, their work at best was pretty and negligible.

Handel has been accused of killing English song. He did nothing of the kind. He recreated it in his own works as far as his imperfect perception of words allowed and his magnificent conception of music directed. He could do no more and no less. If Purcell had come after Handel instead of before him, had been the inheritor of all that Handel revealed of the Italian *cantilena*, and had assimilated its lessons without selling his birthright, the story of English song would have been something very different. But the eighteenth century produced no Purcell. Failing one, England settled down to giving monster performances of Handel's oratorios, trying to persuade other foreign composers to write like him, and trying to believe that its own well-meaning cathedral organists actually did so.

CHAPTER IX
THE BRITISH RENAISSANCE

THE compelling personality of Handel and its outcome in oratorio has carried us far from our main concern, as far indeed as it carried the English people from their native art of song. The digression has been necessary, in order to explain the rudderless condition of British music from the eighteenth century till at any rate late in the nineteenth. In order to recover our standpoint it will be worth while here to summarize the historical sequence which has been traced in former chapters.

The emergence of the vernacular as a vehicle for artistic song came late in England under the influence of Renaissance thought finding vent in the ecclesiastical Reformation. John Merbecke was quick to recognize that the forms and accents of English words and phrases must influence musical rhythms in song. His principles, scarcely regarded in his own day, were abundantly justified in the next generation, which was pre-eminently the era of the madrigal. In the works of Byrd, Weelkes, Gibbons, and others we have an outpouring of lyrical poetry in polyphonic song, each voice pursuing a free rhythm of its own and producing a melody 'framed to the life of the words', as Byrd said. John Dowland at the same time applied the same principle to lyrical solo song accompanied on his lute. The union of voice and verse was complete within certain rather narrow limits. The need for regulating musical ensemble brought the insistence on a recurrent musical accent, and Henry Lawes in his masques succeeded in accommodating verbal accent to this with mechanically satisfactory results. Thus far, up to the date of *Comus* (1634), English song, whether for many voices or for one, for church or home or entertainment, had been purely lyrical. Matthew Locke brought to it the dramatic idea, and, using the technique which Lawes had devised for practical purposes, produced an English style of declamation in strict time, founded on the characteristics of the language in conjunction with the musical recurrent accent. This English declamation is entirely distinct in principle from the Italian recitative. Locke was followed by a man of genius, Henry Purcell, able to wield with consummate ease the tools placed in his hands. We have in the theatre music, church music, odes and songs of Purcell a supple blending of lyrical and dramatic styles, which shows him capable of the highest achievements in the art of song. He needed opportunities which were denied him. He realized that there were aspects of purely musical design which were outside his experience. He tried to master them from the example of the few and imperfect Italian sonatas which reached him. He went far in this direction, but not far enough. Had he been able to travel like Dowland, he might easily have completed his musical education. But he was held at home, he never met a brother artist against whom he could measure his powers, and he died young. Moreover the wish of his heart, and that of his master, Locke, was refused. The London public did not want serious opera; it wanted only a hotch-potch of dramatic and musical entertainment. Purcell was paralysed by a public which had no use for his best. So the English lyric drama was starved to death at the moment when it was needed to fulfil the preparation of over a hundred years. The fruit fell from the tree before it was ripe.

Handel, arriving solely as an adventurous importer of foreign goods, discovered that there had been a native style which he could not wholly understand but which he learnt to respect. He made considerable efforts to recover it even while he was further blinding the public to its possibilities by the brilliance of his importation of Italian opera. Ultimately he became imbued with that spirit of compromise which is itself a typically

English characteristic. He threw over the stage and the Italian singers; he adopted the English language and the English chorus; he produced an unacted quasi-opera which got vitality from its association with familiar themes capable of stirring the imagination of its hearers. In this medium he could rise to a mood of epic grandeur which made his audience oblivious of any incidental maltreatment of their language. He could take the thought from words and wing it away into a purely musical sphere.

But when this epic manner without the epic mind or the musical genius to support it became the daily fare of English musical life, the oratorio form became a disaster. It reached its lowest depths in the middle of the nineteenth century when a composer wrote an oratorio on the subject of Ruth, of which an outstanding feature was a palsied fugal chorus to the words 'And his name was Boas'. There was little or nothing to set against the false Handelian oratorio. English opera in the hands of men like Arne, who had a spark of genius, and Bishop, who had a rushlight of talent, was never allowed to be anything but a series of more or less pretty tunes set to more or less trivial and sentimental verses. In the Shakespearian songs of Arne, the cheerful ballads of Shield, Dibdin, and such worthies, the fraternal relationship between 'music and sweet poetrie' became middle-aged. They kept up a friendly acquaintance for old sake's sake; neither meant very much to the other.

As we contemplate this dismal state of things there is at least a grain of comfort to be extracted from the thought that the loosening of the bonds between music and language was not confined to England. A partial submergence of the vernacular is as characteristic of the eighteenth century as the emergence was of the sixteenth. The Italian opera gained something of the dominance over the whole of musical Europe that the Latin of the medieval church had held two centuries earlier. Its sway extended outside of Italy from Vienna to St. Petersburg.

Only Paris stood out for a native opera founded on the vernacular, and the Parisians who withstood the onslaught of the foreign language and the foreign style of music had to fight out the famous controversy known to history as the *Guerre des Bouffons*. When their own composers failed they called in a great German, Christopher Gluck, to come and vindicate their language in song. The contrast between the stories of Gluck in Paris and of Handel in London is an illuminating one. French opera was enriched by the one, English opera obliterated by the other; but it was not the actions of the individuals so much as the attitudes of the two publics towards their native traditions of art, which caused the difference.

Furthermore the Italian opera, which occupied all the opera-houses of Europe other than that of Paris, was of a type which tended to the submergence again of even its own language. Its strings of arias in stereotyped musical styles were arranged with little regard to dramatic propriety and every regard to the display of vocal virtuosity. A few lines of verse afforded a minimum of verbal content on which the singer might vocalize. Monteverdi's fervent dramatic speech was a thing of the far-distant past. Gluck, knowing nothing of Monteverdi, produced his own *Orfeo* in Vienna (1766) in order to restore a lost ideal. He was too soon, and the *opera seria*, with its ever-increasing musical elaboration at the expense of drama and words, was to continue its course unchecked for another generation.

Meantime the sonata, the symphony, and kindred instrumental forms were growing and proving the self-existent powers of music. The latter part of the eighteenth century from J. S. Bach to Mozart was essentially the period of pure instrumental music in these forms, which, as I suggested in the first chapter, had their roots in the antecedent vocal forms. In order to see that illus-

The British Renaissance

trated in the music of the time you have only to take the pianoforte sonatas of Mozart and compare them with the arias and *ensemble* movements of his Italian operas. You will find that not only the general lay-out or pattern (including the key system) is similar, but that innumerable details, curves of melody, ornaments, &c., are transferred from the voice of the singer to the hand of the player. It was in Mozart's day, too, that the pianoforte definitely superseded the harpsichord, because of its power of producing a 'singing' tone.

The process is logical. Where words are foreign and therefore not wholly intelligible either to composer or audience, the composer is led to concentrate his energies on making his music completely satisfactory in itself; words then become superfluous; he discards them together with the voice itself and carries out his design on instruments: the pianoforte, the string quartet, or the orchestra.

That happened on a small scale in England at the end of the Latin era, when Morley distinguished music as either written on a ditty or without a ditty, and 'In Nomine' and fantasy grew out of the motet; it happened on a much larger scale in Vienna at the end of the Italian era, when the sonata and symphony were born. If it is asked why there was no corresponding instrumental period in England in the eighteenth century, the answer is because the dramatic period had been nipped in the bud. England had set its face against native opera. The divorce of music from language had come too soon and produced sterility.

What is called the Romantic Movement on the Continent at the beginning of the nineteenth century was, so far as it concerned music, primarily a second emergence of the vernacular. We see the thing happening before our eyes in the symphonies of Beethoven. He wrote eight and had actually set sail in a still greater venture in the ninth when he found that he could not compass its course with the instruments alone. His instruments strove for vocal utterance till at last, with a gesture of impatience, he turned to the human voice.

O Freunde, nicht diese Töne

ushers in the vocal ode to Joy. Beethoven wrote clumsily, even badly for the voices, but he had to have them, not as extra instruments, but for their contribution of the burning power of words, and still more for their expression of human personality in the dual act of song.

Meanwhile Schubert, living obscurely in Vienna, had discovered for himself German lyric poetry. Every poem called out a song from him; every song took its shape from the poet's verse. Mood, lilt, and accent of the verse were accommodated in his vocal melody; his pianoforte was for him what the lute had been for Dowland, an instrument capable of participating in personal interpretation with the voice through its susceptibility to subtle lights and shades of phrasing. (See p. 55.) Its greater power and scope, however, made it something more. Schubert's pianoforte accompaniments enlarged on picturesque or descriptive details of the poem; the battering storm through which father and child fight their way and encounter the Erlking, the whirr of Gretchen's spinning-wheel, the trout rising in the pool, the babbling brook and the turning mill-wheel, the wheezy grind of the hurdy-gurdy. In these and innumerable other cases some definite figure in the pianoforte part makes the picture in sound evoked by the poem. Elsewhere the pianoforte's contribution is less objective and is merged in the broader emotional mood of the poem. Whatever the treatment may be, the verbal picture passes through the voice to the instrument. In a few cases, the 'Trout' quintet and the Wanderer Fantasia (pianoforte solo), Schubert completes the circle in his own work by developing the poetic idea in a purely instrumental design. It was Schubert's example more than any other which im-

The British Renaissance 141

pelled Liszt at a later date towards the invention of the 'Symphonic Poem'.

Berlioz, because of his great command of the orchestra, is thought of chiefly as an instrumental composer, yet it was Romantic literature which set him on a path parallel with that of Liszt, and his dissatisfaction with the purely formal side of music and his insistence on its union with ideas capable of verbal expression makes him typical of the general reaction.

Contemporary with the Ninth Symphony of Beethoven and the songs of Schubert comes Weber propagating German opera in *Der Freischütz*, and a little later Glinka devising the Russian opera and Smetana the Czech. Then Wagner's genius, overshadowing the others, carried German opera to undreamed of heights, his majestic style based solely on truthful expression of the language. Brahms found 'new paths' for the sonata and the symphony in the light of that outpouring of native song which had begun with Schubert.

Compared with all this, that which has been called the British Musical Renaissance seems a small and hesitant movement. It came late, it was largely a reflection of what was going on all over the Continent, but it was real and, viewed as a second emergence of the vernacular, it was native born.

Within the lifetime of those of us who even now are not aged there have been three chronological groups at work, who might almost be called three musical generations of British composers, and who have led and participated in this Renaissance.

I wish to be quite clear about this because the term 'Renaissance' in this connexion has been so much abused, especially by journalists, a well-intentioned fraternity of whom I am proud to be one. As each group, almost as each member of each group, has asserted ability in some work of consequence, newspaper articles have been poured out declaring that at last a prophet has arisen and that a Renaissance of

British music is beginning or about to begin. The bewildered onlooker gets the impression that music in this country is always on the eve of some wonderful change, that unmusical people are going to be made musical, and that the millennium will shortly arrive.

This is not the intention of the writers; it is the inevitable result of the tendency fostered by an enterprising Press to regard daily happenings as events of epoch-making importance. If we glance back over the last fifty years with something of that historical perspective which we have tried to bring to our study of other epochs, we can distinguish these groups and observe that a Renaissance began with the first of them.

Taking a dozen names, and choosing them more for the impression they have made on the musical life of the country than for individual attainments, we may make an outline of the groups as follows:

(1) Arthur Sullivan, Hubert Parry, C. V. Stanford, Alexander Mackenzie.
(2) Edward Elgar, Frederick Delius, Granville Bantock, Ethel Smyth.
(3) Vaughan Williams, Gustav Holst, Rutland Boughton, John Ireland.

The importance of several names in the second and third groups may be questioned and there will be some who would wish to substitute others for them. About the first there can be no question; they were the men who brought their art back to the test of the language and, looking to the habits and traditions of people united by the use of a common language, began again to found a musical style in consonance with those habits and traditions. It is significant that the group includes Sullivan, a Londoner of Irish descent; Parry, a west-country Englishman with some Welsh blood in his veins; Stanford, an out-and-out Irishman, though of the English pale; Mackenzie, a Scotsman born and bred. No more thoroughly British quartet could well be found,

The British Renaissance

even though two of them (Sullivan and Stanford) completed their musical education in Germany and Mackenzie spent much of his early life in Italy.

It is the fashion of the history books to date this Renaissance from the appearance of Parry's first important work for solo voices, choir, and orchestra, the *Scenes from Prometheus Unbound* given at Gloucester in 1880. That, as the work which first showed the imaginative power of the man who did most to bring great poetry back into choral song, makes an obviously outstanding date. A humbler event five years earlier was undoubtedly much more powerful in its effect on the public at large, a simple and absurd little one-act opera, which did not claim the title but was described as a 'musical extravaganza', *Trial by Jury*, by W. S. Gilbert and Arthur Sullivan.

Sullivan's part in the Renaissance has never had full justice done to it by people who think that a composer must be judged by the size of his scores and the seriousness of his aims. The post-Handelian oratorio composers had written large enough scores in all conscience, and their seriousness was only too painfully apparent. Sullivan and indeed all the members of this group were hampered by the tradition of self-conscious seriousness which results in pomposity, and Sullivan must not be judged by his oratorio *The Golden Legend* and his 'Grand' opera *Ivanhoe* any more than by such fatuous sentimentalities as 'The Lost Chord' and 'The Chorister'.

There are those who still think that because Sullivan turned out some perfunctory and insincere work he was a second-rate artist. If the test were applied all round we might say 'who then can be saved?' Sullivan was in fact the most spontaneous melodist (if nothing more) that England has produced since Purcell. His defects are largely those that we have recognized in Purcell: they resulted from having to accept uncongenial conditions and serve vulgar tastes in church, drawing-room, and provincial festival. In the theatre he was at home, and in the theatre he found what Purcell never had, collaboration with an ideal librettist (W. S. Gilbert) and manager (D'Oyly Carte), who together were strong enough to insist on proper presentation of the series now known as 'Savoy Operas', from *The Sorcerer* to *The Gondoliers*. Gilbert and Sullivan, therefore, are the one bright spot in the history of British opera, though even here it must be noted that the little preliminary *Trial by Jury* is the only one of the famous series which Purcell would have described as a 'perfect opera', a story told and acted entirely to music; their spoken dialogue evaded the problem of English declamation which Locke and Purcell had solved together two hundred years earlier.

Sullivan had the luck to fall in with a man who understood his generation, who could laugh at it and make his countrymen laugh with him at themselves, their most cherished institutions, their fashions, and their foibles. English music had not laughed since the days of *The Beggar's Opera*. It had wellnigh forgotten the way till Sullivan came. While Gilbert's jingles carried jibes, Sullivan rippled with good-tempered merriment. Their audiences never discovered how cynical Gilbert's humour could be because Sullivan's music kept it sweet. They have not yet discovered Sullivan's genius for language in song, because they still think that it is Gilbert who keeps them amused. Any one who takes the trouble to go through the Savoy Operas, noting Gilbert's repetition of poetic metres, will soon discover how Sullivan saved him from the charge of monotony by the wealth of his musical ideas and variety of his rhythms. There can be no question that it is Sullivan rather than Gilbert who makes these works appeal nowadays to a generation who have hardly heard of the Aesthetic movement of the eighties, who take little interest in the House of Lords, to whom swearing in the Navy is not a serious social abuse, and Japan no longer a funny country where the men carry fans.

The British Renaissance

Even so great an achievement as the creation of a type of comic opera in a series of little masterpieces, each complete in its own genre, could not suffice in itself to produce that general change of outlook in the artists and in their public which deserves the name of a Renaissance. The other members of the group contributed in their own ways and approached the problem each from his own standpoint. Their individual genius for composition is still debated. It has been said that a great part of Stanford's symphonic music is a rather pale copy of Brahms, that Mackenzie's concertos and rhapsodies owe a good deal to Liszt, and that Parry certainly took a considerable time to shake himself free of the Handel-Mendelssohn tradition in which he had been brought up, if indeed he ever did so completely.

Alexander Mackenzie, the only one of the group still living, and a man whom all honour and ought to honour, was brought up as a violinist in Edinburgh and so, coming to music through the instrument rather than the voice, was less fitted than the other two to take a lead in this particular work of the reunion of voice and verse. He certainly had neither the fine literary sense of Stanford nor the instinct for verbal values in sound which made Parry a late successor to Purcell. But he loved his country and his country's traditional song, and he made that love felt in such things as 'The Cotter's Saturday Night', the Scottish Concerto (pianoforte), and the still popular Britannia Overture. The last has the same kind of sea-flavour which Sullivan used so happily in *H.M.S. Pinafore*, but it is employed with more serious intent.

In his choral works and his operas Mackenzie was unfortunate in his librettos. He too readily accepted the hackwork of men like Joseph Bennett and Francis Hueffer, from whom nothing distinguished could come, but his general attitude towards the composer's art was free and generous and opposed to the academicism which had tethered it hitherto to the organ stool and the oratorio. As a teacher, and especially as head of the Royal Academy of Music, Mackenzie did a great and reviving work.

Charles Villiers Stanford made his way back to native song through the German song of Brahms and Schubert. He grasped the fact that they were what they were, because their melody had sprung from the soil and was rooted in the folk-melody belonging to their own language. He got down to bedrock when he steeped himself in Irish folk-song as preserved in Moore's Irish Melodies and the great collection of Edward Bunting, which he edited. It would be unwise to attempt to say how far he was guided by pure intuition and how far by intellectual reasoning through a process of conscious synthesis following on analysis.

It is beyond question that he re-discovered an idiom in traditional Irish melody allied to English poetry which became a part of himself. His many exquisite songs, notably those of the cycles 'Cushendall' and 'A Fire of Turf', exhibit a blend of whimsical humour, pathos, and tenderness that make them as complete an expression of the Anglo-Irish temperament as Schubert's were of the Austro-German. Every one who has heard Mr. Plunket Greene sing 'The fairy Lough', 'Cuttin' Rushes', 'The Grace for Light', 'Grandeur', will realize this, and also the extraordinary suppleness of the music to the form of each poem.

Both Stanford and Mackenzie were protagonists in the campaign, unsuccessful up to the present, to establish a native opera, and both of them devoted themselves to operatic composition to a remarkable extent considering the slight opportunity for performance which the country afforded. That has been the most uphill task both for them and their successors. Their countrymen have been content to observe that not one of them is either a Verdi, a Wagner, or a Puccini, and, having done so, to return to those masters, either sung by

The British Renaissance

foreigners in their original language or by English singers in translations. When a British composer can do better than the best foreign operas his countrymen will be glad to hear him; not till then: that is the general attitude. The question is, would a British audience be able to recognize the wonder if it were offered them? By what standards could it be judged, seeing the obliviousness to the subtleties of the language in song under which English music has laboured for so long?

Stanford, indeed, in the course of many efforts, did achieve one charming little opera of Irish life, *Shamus O'Brien*, which might have taken a foundational place in a British repertory similar to that of Smetana's *Bartered Bride* in the Czech repertory. It was produced in London shortly after the series of the Savoy Operas had been completed. It was every bit as genial in its melody and as delicate in its orchestration as *The Yeomen of the Guard*, but as it had not the Gilbertian humour it was admired during a short run and then dropped.

Hubert Parry tilled a more fruitful field, that of concert works for choir and orchestra. A man of remarkable intellectual and physical energy, brought up in the tradition of English country life, with the addition of public school and university, Eton and Oxford, his background was that of the typical Englishman of the upper classes, to which he brought something of his own and which was anything but typical of his class, an instinct and serious regard for fine quality in the arts. A lover of athletic exercise rather than of sport, a voracious reader, a student of history, politics and social problems, he brought all these many-sided interests to bear on the devotion of his life, the art of music.

He was still quite a young man when the splendours of the Wagnerian music-drama burst on an astonished and bewildered world. England in the seventies looked askance at Wagner as the leader of a dangerous revolutionary movement, which not only turned the arts topsy-turvy but seemed to have its roots in subversive doctrines inimical to organized religion and other cherished institutions of a respectable society. The very name *Götterdämmerung* had an ominous sound; the stories of Siegfried and Sieglinde, Tristan and Isolde, extolled most undesirable things. Of course opera was always apt to be a little immoral, but no one took seriously *La Traviata* and *Rigoletto*; sensible people just listened to Patti and forgot about the stories, while apparently you were meant to take Wagner's reprobates seriously. This was the general tone of society, particularly that section of it to which Parry belonged. He saw right through it and through all the confusion of thought which Wagner's written utterances and the muddleheadedness of his admirers were calculated to produce. He got straight to the essence of the thing, realized what Wagner's art meant to the world, and struck out for personal freedom of thought and action.

Though Parry drank in Wagner's artistic philosophy he never succumbed to it as weaker minds have done. He did not sit down to write ponderous music dramas on legendary subjects, as the Wagnerian copyists in England as well as Germany did. He was clearer than any of his contemporaries about the basic fact that when an artist has done a thing supremely well merely to try to do it too is banal and foolish. Almost all the leaders of the British Renaissance have yielded to this temptation in varying degrees and acting on different examples. Parry never yielded to it one inch. As life went on he refused current fashions in musical expression with an increasing asceticism of taste, and preferred to be cold-shouldered by those who partook of them rather than write with an eye to immediate effect, which would have been insincere in him. He who had imbibed Wagner's message when it was obscure to the rest of his world was later despised by a public who had discovered the attractiveness of Wagner's glowing orchestration.

The British Renaissance 149

While the enthusiasm for Wagner was still hot on him, Parry wrote a letter to a friend which clearly showed that he had no intention of echoing the master. He recognized that his own problems were something entirely different. In his first choral work, *Scenes from Prometheus Unbound* (1880), he found in Shelley's drama something of the spiritual revolt which had fired him in Wagner. In the musical handling of that beautiful work there are distinct traces of Wagner's method, but they are slight and they were soon outgrown in later ones. As he went further he found his own philosophy of life embodied in English literature, particularly in the majestic prose of the English Bible and the sonorous measure of Milton's verse. The ode 'Blest Pair of Sirens' for double chorus and orchestra, still his most famous work, arrived in 1887. It followed on a setting of James Shirley's 'The Glories of our Blood and State'.

When he took up oratorio with the composition of *Judith* (1889), those who had watched Parry's early progress with understanding were inclined to fear, not without reason, that in returning to that much-abused form he was falling a prey to what had remained of the post-Handelian tradition. *Judith*, indeed, and its successor *King Saul*, have a good many of the defects of that style, but neither was approached in the unthinking spirit which had pervaded the English oratorio. As a short preface to the former shows, the composer wished to centralize the interest on 'popular movements and passions', and he did in fact achieve something of that epic breadth which had belonged to Handel at his best. What he tried for imperfectly in these two oratorios he achieved in the last work of the kind, *Job* (1892), the whole design and execution of which is illumined by the idea of enlightenment and spiritual enrichment through suffering, treated with an extraordinary intimacy combined with dignity. The lamentation of Job is one of the greatest declamatory solos in the language. Parry's unswerving seriousness of purpose made certain critics who had at first derided him give him the sobriquet of 'the English Bach'. It was a double-edged compliment, and probably meant to be one, since men like Joseph Bennett, who was primarily responsible for it, understood and cared for Bach as little as they understood and cared for Parry and his music. It was quite inappropriate and meaningless. If they had called him the 'nineteenth-century Purcell' there would have been some sense in their nickname, but they knew too little of Purcell even to think of the phrase.

Parry had neither the inventive resource nor the light-hearted adaptability of Purcell, but he had his sensitiveness to language, and added to it a fineness of taste and judgement in his choice of words which belonged to him as a man of cultivation living in a more enlightened age than that of Purcell. Parry's poets were Shakespeare (four sonnets and other songs), Milton ('Blest Pair', 'L'Allegro', and 'Il Penseroso'), Shelley ('Prometheus'), Tennyson ('The Lotus-Eaters'); though in later years he chose some small lyrics by minor poets for his songs, he was as incapable of setting rubbish as Purcell was powerless to resist it.

Both in poetry and in prose Parry evolved for himself a style of melodic declamation which is similar in principle to Purcell's. In later years he was a serious student of Purcell,[1] but he certainly did not consciously form his own style on Purcell's example. He had indeed arrived at English declamation through Wagner, just as Stanford arrived at lyric song through Brahms and Schubert. His likeness to Purcell is due rather to the discovery that Purcell's way was *the* way.

Two samples may be quoted here merely as suggestions of how the likeness may be traced. One from 'L'Allegro' shows a rhythmical treatment of verse

[1] See *Oxford History of Music*. 'The Seventeenth Century', by C. H. H. Parry.

The British Renaissance

identical with that which Purcell understood and used in *Dido* and Handel misunderstood in *Theodora* (see examples on p. 117). The other is taken from that last series of cantatas (not oratorios) on words from the Bible which illustrate from several points of view Parry's ultimate philosophy of life. The passage itself is chosen merely for its accentual treatment of words in a strict-time declamation like Purcell's. It is followed in the cantata by a chorus, 'To everything there is a season', which deserves to be studied as an example of the choral solution of a similar verbal problem, but still more for its beauty and for the return which it makes to serenity of spirit after the dark pessimism of the solo preceding it.

Parry. (' L'Allegro. ')

Some-time walk-ing, not.. un-seen, By hedge-row elms, on hil-locks green.

And, be-hold.. all was van-i-ty, van-i-ty, van-i-ty and vex-a-tion of

The whole series of Parry's last cantatas should be studied in conjunction with Purcell's anthems. Though Parry was the more profound thinker and Purcell the more original genius, they have a community of feeling and expression, rooted as they are in the same language, which is quite unlike any continental art form. At the end of the nineteenth century Parry recovered for English song what it had lost with the death of Purcell two hundred years before.

CHAPTER X
OPEN QUESTIONS

WHAT next? We might devote the last pages to a study of the oratorios of Elgar, the choral symphonies of Vaughan Williams and Holst, the operas of Delius, Ethel Smyth, Rutland Boughton, and others of the later groups who have contributed to that Renaissance which Sullivan, Parry, and their contemporaries began. A study of living British composers would be a subject fit to fill a whole course of ten lectures, and I hope that a subsequent Cramb lecturer may undertake it. It would be, however, as irrelevant to my purpose here as it would be necessarily inadequate at this stage of our discussion.

Instead of embarking on it I prefer to touch on some questions which are constantly asked, suggest my own answer to them, and encourage others to find theirs. Some of these questions are frequently hurled at one's head in a way which makes it impossible to answer them; as when a neighbour at dinner suddenly says, 'What do you think of this modern music?' or, 'English is so bad for singing, isn't it?' Others are earnestly asked by anxious parents who say, 'My daughter has such a lovely voice; do you think it would be best to send her to Italy to study?' or, 'Do tell me, who is really the best singing-teacher in London?' Or perhaps the questions are raised in the form of a horrified statement by a paterfamilias or a business man: 'Music is all very well, but you can't possibly spend public money on it. Look at the rates and the income-tax!'

Does our talk of Purcell and Handel and the English language in song bear at all on such questions as these? It seems remote enough from some of them, but I think it underlies the answers to them all.

Most of us who have watched the progress of the British Renaissance in music with any closeness have a disquieting feeling that it has not quite fulfilled itself. We have seen composers with the most promising talents becoming in middle age teachers, concert-givers, propagandists—anything and everything but creative artists. We say we are a musical country, yet concert-giving institutions have to struggle for existence, to repeat over and over the most popular works, and frequently reduce the number of their concerts. We see opera companies going into liquidation or just avoiding doing so by wearily touring the provinces with a small repertory of hackneyed foreign works.

The musical colleges are seething with clever young people—composers, singers, players, who fade away and are forgotten when their training is over. 'British music' has become a slogan which arouses the utmost enthusiasm, yet nine-tenths of the music by British-born composers bears practically no mark of its country of origin, and when the public gets an opera like *Hugh the Drover*, which is rooted in its own folk-song and folk-lore, it hears it a few times as a curiosity and soon returns to *La Bohème* or *Der Rosenkavalier*.

Choral singing is fostered and brought to a level of performance far above that of most continental countries, but that is done largely by arousing the spirit of competition between choirs, and meantime solo singing gets worse and worse. Those which remain of the old provincial festivals frequently show us the spectacle of incompetent solo singers being rapturously applauded by members of a highly trained amateur choir who alone were responsible for whatever was good in the performance.

These anomalies seem mainly due to one cause. The British public is a horse which always refuses at a particular fence, the fence of native opera. Many cultured people despise opera altogether. One may partly sympathize with those who say, 'If I want a play I go to the theatre; if music, I go to a concert.' One may wholly sympathize with those who say that the opera has been responsible for more bad art than any other institution in the world except the Christian Church. Nevertheless opera is essential, because it is the only means through which the union of language and music can be effected and developed to the full in song, and only through that union does a nation evolve a distinctive musical style of its own.

The French, who established the Comédie Française and the Académie de Musique side by side in the seventeenth century, developed traditions both of dramatic speech and of vocal declamation in song which were able to withstand every attack from without, and while French music to-day is as various as that which is included under the names of Fauré, Massenet, Debussy, and Ravel, there can never be any doubt that these composers and a dozen others are really French in their outlook. Recognizable attributes of the French character are stamped on all their work, both vocal and instrumental.

I am far from wishing to suggest that what the French have done we should do, that we should seek to establish our musical identity by following even the most excellent of foreign examples. The logical Latin mind creates an institution for the cultivation of an art and cultivates till the plant grows, blossoms, and bears fruit. The less logical British mind leaves the arts to grow wild. We say that we believe in private enterprise and mistrust State direction, but in that case it is time that we brought private enterprise to bear on this particular problem. Private enterprise has for the most part produced our musical schools, beginning with the Royal Academy of Music in London just over a hundred years ago, and very fine they are. Glasgow is even now considering plans for the enlargement of this very lectureship into a professorship carrying with it the headship of a Scottish school of music.

Schools to train young artists are necessary things, but for what are the young to be trained? They are to compose, sing, and play, but what are they to compose, and where are they to perform?

The answer at present is, they are to compose whatever they like and perform it wherever they can. The bigger their aim the smaller is their chance of a hearing. The writer of pretty little songs may still make a hit at the Ballad Concerts, though even these are dwindling; the composer of an orchestral piece (preferably one not taking more than ten minutes in performance) may get it played at the London Promenade Concerts, at Bournemouth, Manchester, or perhaps by the Scottish Orchestra. These are institutions which have done much for native orchestral music. The only trouble with them is that there are not enough of them and that their position is not sufficiently assured to enable them to take risks. The composer of choral music on a large scale used to find some opportunity at the provincial festivals and in the larger choral societies. That opportunity is now much diminished. At their best all these things can only provide occasional and intermittent engagements to composers, singers, and players. The only institution which could provide a goal for their studentship, a living for their working years, and above all a standard of criticism for artists and audiences alike, is a native opera. That has been refused and, so far as one can see, will be refused by the public, which continues to found music schools and to tempt young people into what is called the 'musical profession' by the offer of free scholarships at those schools, with no regard to the prospects or the quality of their work in after-life.

The Royal College of Music in London was founded at the beginning of that period which has been described as the British Musical Renaissance. It and its sister colleges have done their work only too well. We have the composers, the singers, and the players, no established outlet for their energies, and no definite criterion by which their attainments can be tested. Sir

Open Questions

Charles Stanford, himself most active in the cause of the Royal College of Music and probably the greatest teacher of composition in England since William Byrd, foresaw[1] from the first the fallacy underlying this Renaissance fever for musical education, and worked unceasingly to convince others of the need for that extra-mural education which only a national opera can give to both artists and audiences. He and others like him were disregarded, and exactly the consequence which they foresaw is now taking place. The fruits of the Renaissance are decaying just as they did at the time of the death of Henry Purcell. The union of language and music in song cannot consolidate into a recognizable native type of art. Highly trained artists pick up precarious livings in restaurants and theatre bands,[2] and the system of training in the schools is necessarily desultory and haphazard.

Next to the composers, who go on writing operas in the dark, as it were, with the knowledge that the chances of a performance are a hundred to one against them, the singers are the most adversely affected by this state of things. Can it be wondered that solo singing gets worse and worse when neither teacher nor pupil has any definite objective towards which to direct the training. Let us come back to the case of the young lady with the lovely voice whose anxious parent says, 'Shall I send my daughter to Italy?' The answer is, 'Certainly, Madam, if you think your daughter likely to become a *prima donna* of the Italian operatic stage.' British singers, male and female, are at the present time and as a result of foreign training holding leading positions in the best opera-houses of Europe. With that training

---

[1] See *Studies and Memories*. 'The Case for a National Opera', by C. V. Stanford.

[2] Cinemas and wireless broadcasting no doubt help to make those livings less precarious; they may provide daily bread for the artists and entertainment for audiences, but cannot affect the larger artistic question favourably.

the cosmopolitan musical life of Europe and America is open to them, and some of them prove themselves as good as the best.[1] The Royal Academy of Music and the Royal College of Music are not supplying singers to the opera-houses of Europe. They cannot give the kind of training needed for such work for obvious reasons. They could give the kind of training needed for the singing of English in opera and concert-room.

But if the young lady with the lovely voice comes to one of them, what does she get? A little operatic work in case an opening should occur for her either in one of the spasmodic attempts to encourage British opera or in light opera, musical comedy, or even revue; some acquaintance with oratorio in case the Three Choirs or the Royal Choral Society should give her a chance in *Elijah*, a smattering of cosmopolitan music.

Then an English singer must know languages. Perhaps she will come out at a song recital. It will not pay, of course, but the agents say she must have Press notices. She must show that she can sing in Italian, German, and French; old Italian songs for the *bel canto* and the great German classics will serve to placate 'the critics'; something French, and therefore rather more *chic*,—Debussy or Reynaldo Hahn perhaps, may get her a drawing-room engagement, and her programme can be filled up at the end with some of those old English things that she used to sing before she got her training.

I do not mean that these are the ideals of singing teaching at our musical colleges; far from it. They are often accused of having too lofty an ideal, of preparing for work which the young people will never reach when they cease to be young people. No, these are the practical conditions which a singing-teacher, whether on the staff of a musical college or teaching privately,

[1] Since this was written Sir Thomas Beecham has produced his scheme for an Imperial League of Opera. The response has not suggested any general change in the public mind.

Open Questions 159

knows that his pupil will have to face, and in proportion as he tries to make his course practical the repertory which he teaches must be of this ragbag kind. He is also frequently teaching against time, for the lovely voice must begin to prove its loveliness before an audience as soon as possible, and if engagements begin to offer themselves to the promising pupil it is hard to refuse them. They may not come again.

The British-trained singer then starts on his or her career with a hastily acquired technique and at best a rough working knowledge of how to interpret a number of different styles of music, most of them foreign ones. The chief virtue in this equipment is a readiness to take up any sort of music in any language, known or unknown, and make something of it at short notice. The British-trained singer is generally a 'quick study'. After a few years of this jack-of-all-trades life the hastily acquired 'method' breaks down, the voice shows signs of wear, and the singer has no settled style to compensate for the increasing vocal defect.

The case of the British-born singer trained abroad is not much happier if he comes back to sing in his own country. I remember a case of one, a tenor, who had made a brilliant début on the Italian stage (I think La Scala in Milan), whose performance in Italian opera at Covent Garden created a furore, and who was then engaged to sing in *Elijah* at an English Festival. He sang—

Eef weeth ahl yure haartz ye trooly seek Heem.

He apparently did not know that there were any vowels in the English language other than open ones, or if he knew that they were there, he knew that he could not vocalize on them. He is still famous abroad, but he rarely sings here.

That brings us to another question, more often put as a statement with which instant agreement is expected: 'English is so bad for singing, isn't it?' If it were

'English is so badly sung', one would have to agree with it. It is badly sung because many of the best singing-teachers in the country do not know the language. They speak it themselves with an Italian or German or other alien accent. Their ears cannot tell them when their pupils are singing it correctly. They could not teach it even if they had any inducement to do so, and without any established institution for the singing of the English language they have no inducement and no corrective.

The native teachers know nothing of the classical principles of English declamation in song. They have had no occasion to explore them. Ask any one of them what they know of Purcell, and they will answer that 'Nymphs and Shepherds' is a good song for a soprano and 'Ye twice ten hundred deities' for a bass. If they have ever come near a cathedral choir they will know one or two anthems and hate them. English is badly sung (1) because very few composers know how to set the language to music, and those who do are instantly shelved on the plea that their music, being different in style from foreign music, is necessarily inferior; (2) because the teachers of singing have no knowledge of English music and language and no inducement to acquire a knowledge; (3) because the singers cannot afford to devote the time to study it; it will not pay them to do so.

Is this merely a cynical tirade and a dismal jeremiad? I expect to be told that it is not only that but a complaint of evils long since past, and most unjust to our able and hard-working musicians of every class. Look at the improvement of the last fifty years. Think of the singers of English we have had, such as Agnes Nicholls, Muriel Foster, Gervase Elwes, John Coates, Plunket Greene. Did not these find it worth while to learn to sing the English language, and are not some of them teaching it now? True; it is just because I do look at the improvement of the last fifty years that the need of the present seems to me so pressing and only to be supplied by one thing, that which the British public refuses—the English opera. That group of singers and a number of others with them were the singing counterpart of the Renaissance of English song among composers. They had the songs of Stanford and Parry, the declamatory cantatas of the latter and the oratorios of Elgar to work on. They made their reputations in types of native music which for the moment the British public demanded. The way had been prepared at the end of the nineteenth century, just as it was at the end of the seventeenth century, for the establishment of a British music founded on the language. A permanent institution was needed to consolidate the style. That institution could only be something in the nature of opera, since epic oratorios and contemplative cantatas cannot be the daily fare of a musical people. Such things belong to the exceptional moment, the festival, which is to the musical life what the retreat is to the religious life. Mackenzie, Goring Thomas, Frederic Cowen, wrote operas for the Carl Rosa Company, which, to its credit, produced them as well as it was able; Stanford stormed the foreign citadel of Covent Garden; Sullivan had an opera-house built for his one 'grand' opera; Parry wrote an opera and put it away in a drawer; Elgar turned away from the stage altogether, but his early cantatas, 'King Olaf' and 'Caractacus', would have been better as operas than they were as concert works. Ethel Smyth and Delius looked to the Continent for performance; Rutland Boughton went into the country and tried to make an opera company for himself; Vaughan Williams and Holst wrote operas which got temporary hearing on a wave of post-war nationalist enthusiasm. Through fifty years the British public has said: By all means have composers; by all means train singers, but do not ask us to employ them in the one way which can be permanent.

Native opera, that is Purcell's 'perfect opera', a play

set throughout to music, is the British public's Dr. Fell. The London public will submit to be entertained through a short season by expensive foreigners; the big provincial cities may be cajoled into listening to a few foreign masterpieces translated into English, but there the interest in dramatic music ceases abruptly.

The moment when the institution ought to have been forthcoming and must have produced great results passed. Perhaps it is too late now. I do not think it is, but it certainly soon will be. Without it the work of the British Renaissance must dwindle and die and we must fall back on the first audacious foreigner who comes to claim our allegiance. At present the Continent has not got a Handel to send us; failing one we take all the continental freaks very seriously and imagine that each in turn is some great one.

This reminds me of the question, 'What do you think of this modern music?' I usually parry it with a counter-question, 'What modern music?' That silences the inquirer, who means, but does not know that he (or more frequently she) means, any music not written in the idiom of the last century. Certain works of Byrd and even of Purcell might be included in the category if they were not known to have been written some three hundred years ago. They include melodies not referable to the major and minor scales and harmonic expressions, which are strange to ears accustomed to the German classics ranging from Handel to Brahms. By modern music the inquirer chiefly means music with harmonies which sound odd at a first hearing. The Elizabethan madrigals are full of such harmonies.

But we may let that point pass and admit that since about the year 1900, since Richard Strauss produced *Ein Heldenleben* and Claude Debussy *Pelléas et Mélisande*, music has been exhibiting more and more diversity and oddness in its harmonic expressions, and that even the most decorous of composers to-day uses

Open Questions

combinations of sound which the great revolutionary, Wagner himself, would have regarded as subversive.

Now I hinted at the outset that this modern music can be divided into two classes, that which builds on and extends the forms founded on the vocal scales, out of which all European music of the last thousand years has sprung, and that which rejects these forms and scales as premises. The latter, accepting the instrumental tools (orchestra, pianoforte, harpsichord, &c.) which were devised to extend the European music of harmonized vocal sounds, is trying to invent a new music out of such unvocal noises as these tools are capable of producing. Composers in this sort are rejecting the true vocal scale, to which the tempered scale of the pianoforte is merely an approximation. They think in equal temperament. In this one fact alone they differ from all their predecessors. For them there are no absolute euphonies and therefore no cacophonies. Since an octave has been divided for practical purposes into twelve semitones, it may equally reasonably be divided into eighteen one-third tones or twenty-four quarter tones. The pianoforte is an instrument of percussion: therefore let it hammer out arresting rhythms. The harpsichord has little sustaining power and no emphasis: therefore it is well suited to bring its inexpressiveness to the aid of this unvocal music. The fiddle and the oboe are both dangerously vocal: they have an inherent tendency towards *cantilena*, but they can be made to scrape and shriek.

This seems to be the music of the rubbish heap, but objects of value do sometimes get thrown there, and in this commercial age we have learnt the importance of utilizing the by-products of every type of manufacture. Perhaps these searchers for a new music may find something serviceable on the rubbish heap of the old. At any rate they are quite welcome to go on turning it over on the chance.

But the other class is the one about which we have

to form judgements and draw distinctions, and we may do so just as surely as we can between a sonata of Beethoven and one of Hummel, or a fugue of Bach and one of Fux. There is no question of taking 'this modern music' as a whole or leaving it as a whole. Accustom your ears to the modal melodies of Byrd and the harmonic clashes of Weelkes or of Purcell (the latter generally introduced to give intensity to some dramatic idea expressed in words) and you will find the prototypes of much that the best of our modern British composers are writing to-day. Vaughan Williams's Pastoral Symphony, for example, though written for a modern orchestra, is vocal through and through and entirely in line with that English tradition which we have traced through generations of song. British audiences are only in danger of confounding it with the music which seems eccentric or iconoclastic because they have so completely forgotten their native tradition.

Most of the best things in modern music come from composers who have kept close to their several native traditions, and whose individual genius has enabled them to extend it in directions undreamed of by their predecessors. One thinks of De Falla in Spain, Janacèk in Czecho-Slovakia, Bela Bartók in Hungary, as names which may be put beside that of Vaughan Williams in England. In all of them you may find some unsuccessful experiments, some hint of abnormality, a wilful rejection of accepted conventions. They have all lived through a time of stress and change and the shattering of the old idols, but they have not turned their backs on the old ideals or bowed the knee to the Baal of sensationalism for commercial profit.

Charlatanry in art is no new thing, and we have more of it now than formerly, because notoriety is offered with both hands by international news agencies supplying the needs of an enterprising Press in Europe and America. Granted that nine-tenths of 'this modern music' is merely the outcome of the search for notoriety by mediocre minds, there is still the other tenth, the real 'upper ten' of the art, and it is in the discovery of it, distinguishing it from its inferior surroundings, that we listeners have our opportunity and get our artistic satisfaction.

It is worth noticing, too, that the representatives of this 'upper ten' among composers are for the most part drawn from those countries which have not formerly been prominent in making big music. It is from Berlin, Vienna, and Paris that most of what I have called the rubbish-heap music comes. Having gone through a great period in which the union of music with their languages was consummated in song and opera, and fruitful in symphony and symphonic poem, they are suffering from artistic exhaustion. They are turning over the rubbish heaps of the past and utilizing the by-products.

That, at least, cannot be our case. The country is not musically stale, whatever else it may be. We have had a new birth of the art in contact with the language. We have discovered among the people of the British Isles unsuspected talents both for the making and performance of music. Those talents can be used or stifled. The Renaissance may die of starvation; we are certainly a long way from satiety.

But what I chiefly think of 'this modern music' is that there is no need to get in a fuss about it. Gamaliel was a wise man, and what he said of subversive tenets in religion is equally true of art. The experiments which are no good will drop off quickly enough. It is not true as far as the arts are concerned that 'the evil that men do lives after them'. The evil is certain to find its way to the rubbish heap. The one danger is lest the good should be buried there too, and we English-speaking people have special cause to fear that, because we have allowed it to happen in the past.

The issue then is a simple one. Our glimpse at history, slight though it has necessarily been, has shown how a people's music grows in contact with a people's mother tongue. From the emergence of the vernacular in poetry and prose literature, speech stamps its character with increasing decisiveness on the music of that people. The use of their own language in religious exercises has a far-reaching effect on their music. Drama as the fullest presentation of their life in art gives the richest opportunity for direct expression of emotions through words and music combined in song. They must bring their song into musical drama of some sort (which for convenience we call Opera) if they are to make the most of it. If they refuse to do so at the right time, when conditions are ripe for it, they lose their music as the English did at the end of the seventeenth century and as they are in danger of doing again in the twentieth century.

Dramatic expression of words through song is an essential stage through which a nation's music must pass if it is to maintain its identity. We value French, German, Italian, Russian music because each has maintained its identity and shown itself different from the art of its neighbours. Our neighbours cannot value British music because they cannot find that it has an identity in which it differs from theirs. That is because we have refused to allow it the necessary scope to expand. We have said an emphatic 'no' each time it has approached the dramatic phase of its development, have silenced each composer in turn on the plea that opera is an imperfect form of art and that anyhow foreign composers can do it better. The argument has been that we want very little opera, so let us import that little from the best foreign firm. That may seem commercially sound, but in that case it is not commercially sound to go on creating and enlarging institutions for training composers and performers. If we are not going to have English opera, in the end we are not going to have British music. If we are not going to have British music, it is neither fair to the individuals concerned nor a sound policy for the community to encourage an appreciable proportion of the population, whose talents lie in that direction, to devote their lives to the provision of the unwanted commodity. Sooner or later we shall have to choose; we cannot long halt between two opinions.

www.ingramcontent.com/pod-product-compliance
Lightning Source LLC
Chambersburg PA
CBHW030112170426
43198CB00009B/593